YAHWEH
THE GOD OF THE
OLD TESTAMENT

✠ ✠ ✠ ✠

Robert W. Gleason, SJ

Research Professor
Fordham University

PRENTICE-HALL, INC.   ENGLEWOOD CLIFFS, N.J.

Imprimi potest:

John J. McGinty, SJ
Praep. Prov. Neo Eboracensis
January 1, 1964

Nihil obstat:

Donald A. Panella, STL, SSL
Censor Deputatus

Imprimatur:

✠ Francis Cardinal Spellman
Archbishop of New York
February 5, 1964

The *nihil obstat* and *imprimatur* are official declarations that a book or pamphlet is free of doctrinal or moral error. No implication is contained therein that those who have granted the *nihil obstat* and *imprimatur* agree with the contents, opinions, or statements expressed.

Library of Congress Catalog Card No.: 62-16888

Printed in the United States of America
[97184-C]

PRENTICE-HALL INTERNATIONAL, INC., *London*
PRENTICE-HALL OF AUSTRALIA, PTY., LTD., *Sydney*
PRENTICE-HALL OF CANADA, LTD., *Toronto*
PRENTICE-HALL FRANCE, S.A.R.L., *Paris*
PRENTICE-HALL OF INDIA (PRIVATE) LTD., *New Delhi*
PRENTICE-HALL OF JAPAN, INC., *Tokyo*
PRENTICE-HALL DE MEXICO, S.A., *Mexico City*

CONTENTS

� ✛ ✛ ✛

iii

INTRODUCTION

✠ ✠ ✠ ✠

The Old Testament takes the existence of God as an unquestioned reality. Not even the fool questions or denies this fundamental affirmation. When the fool says in his heart that there is no God, he is not attempting to deny God's existence; he is simply declaring that God chooses not to be involved in our human affairs, or affirming that God's sovereignty does not extend to the fool's life. The fool's life is not structured by the absolute moral imperative of Yahweh's will; his declaration that there is no God is a declaration of a refusal to submit to this will and not a denial of God's existence.

God's existence is simply beyond question or proof. In general, the Old Testament does not even attempt to prove the existence of God. When the sacred authors describe the marvels of God's creation, it is not to establish the fact that God exists, but to offer an occasion for His praise, to describe His being and His deeds. There are passages in the Old Testament which offer the basis for a rational proof of God's existence (notably Wisd. of Sol. 13:1-9), but these passages usually intend to emphasize one or more aspects of God's nature rather than His

1

existence. The emphasis here is on the fact that Yahweh is the *real* God.

All of nature knows God; even the pagans have some knowledge of Him, and Israel has the knowledge born of experience of God, of revelation. God has communicated with Israel by speech. Israel knows Him, and here knowledge is used not as a speculative admission of a truth of the theoretical order, but as a living obedience to the moral will of Yahweh. To know God is to accept His goodness, His sovereignty, and the moral demands made upon us by His Lordship in the existential order. It is only when the prophets are engaged in polemics against false gods that they stress the existence of God, and here the note underscored is less the fact that Yahweh *is* than that He is unique and the other gods are nonexistent. To know Yahweh is to recognize Him for *what* He is, to submit in fear and love to His demands, to do Him the homage of obedience, to grasp something of His nature as He has revealed it in His mighty deeds and in His speech to men.

The sinner may be said not to "know" God for he resists His will, and yet even the sinner declares the existence of God, for his sin consists precisely in his revolt or rebellion against God. Every man is constituted in a relationship of service to God, and the sinner is one who refuses to fulfill his duties. He is a man in rebellion against a living and present Person.

If we can call the man who lives as if God did not exist a practical atheist, then the Old Testament knows of atheism. But speculative atheism is as foreign to its thought as is speculative demonstration of God's existence. The reality of God is absolutely primordial; He is there from the beginning as a living force in life. Israel's neighbors may discuss the birth of their gods; Israel does not. He was from the beginning, and there is no trace in the Old Testament of the evolution of God or of a battle of the gods or of God against chaos, although there are *literary reminiscences* of such battle myths in Job and the Psalms.

Because of Israel's profound conviction of the living character of her God, the Old Testament abounds with anthropomorphisms. Her God is a concrete power, active in the history of the world and of Israel. Knowledge of Him does not come from reflection but from His speech and action. He is active and personal, and He lets Himself be known by Israel as an accessible God, intervening in life and history. The Old Testament, as a result, often speaks of God as if He were a man. It speaks of His hands, His fingers, His arms, His back, His eyes, His nostrils. He walks in the garden of Eden; He listens, He smells, He speaks; He comes down to Babel; He works as a potter; He whistles and laughs; He treads the wine press; and He closes the door of the Ark after Moses. He is a valiant warrior, like a roaring lion. He feels jealousy and wrath and joy and contentment, even repentance. The concrete way in which God is spoken of suits both the genius of the Hebrew language and Israel's profound conviction that God is personal, fully alive. He is transcendent and yet immanent to history. Although Israel acknowledges that God is eternal, she does not affirm this as a fact of primary concern. Since He possesses the plenitude of life, there is no period when He was not living, but eternity is not subject to much speculation in the Old Testament. Yahweh may be spoken of in terms that befit man, for He is fully personal, but His sanctity is such that He never assumes the all-too-human characteristics of the gods of pagan mythology. Even when He deals most familiarly with Israel, He remains the "wholly Other."

Some authorities have suggested that the expression the "living God" is of relatively late date in Israel's literature and sprang from the polemics with the pagan gods who were supposed to die and be reborn each year. But the idea certainly seems to be ancient in Israel since one of the commonest oaths was to swear by the living God (I Sam. 14:39, 17:36, 19:6; Jud. 8:19). Yahweh Himself uses the expression when He wishes to confirm His statements or His threats (Ezek. 17:19).

Yahweh demonstrates that He is a living God by freeing Israel from the threats of enemies. In contrast to the living God

of Israel, the gods of her neighbors are utterly lifeless and im-
potent, unable to save their worshippers. The God of Israel is
the ruler of nature and nations, a power whom Israel has experienced as Savior and Judge, involved in all the details of
personal and natural life. History is subject to His action, and
the life of the people is involved in His vital acts of destroying
and building, delivering and judging. He is transcendent, the
wholly Other, and yet present, in immediate relationship to
man.

Scholars debate which aspect of the divine being should be
most underscored in dealing with the subject of God. Some
have centered their treatment around His Holiness or His being
alive or His being accessible and present, or transcendent,
secret, hidden, and unique. It is hardly possible to give pref-
erence to any of these aspects since only their unity can express
something of God's nature.

One point upon which all scholars agree is that Israel's idea
of God is wholly different from the conceptions of the deities
prevalent among her neighbors. Her neighbors' gods were
visible and tangible; it is completely alien to the Old Testament
to make an image of God, or *any* image, for that matter. Over
and over again it is stated that God enters into communion
with man, yet God is asserted to be invisible, incomparable,
hidden. His spiritual goodness, His mercy, His activity in history
are stressed, but His being stays hidden. No creed is drawn up
to express His attributes or describe His being. The gods of
the other Semites could be placated by magic. In none of the
literature did the official religion teach that one could con-
strain Yahweh, whose liberty was unassailable and, in fact, un-
predictable. The gods of her neighbors promised plenty and
affluence, fertility and material abundance. Israel's God was
mysterious: He imposed his moral will for man's good, but
often the aims He had in mind were not the goals the Hebrew
would have naturally chosen.

The gods of her neighbors were essentially unprincipled;
Yahweh was unspeakably holy. He was entirely different from

what Israel would have made Him if left to herself. He pours out blessings, but He also sends suffering and affliction—even to the just man, as Job noted.

An immediate communion is possible between God and man, but only because God has so chosen. One can speak to him familiarly. This presence is the basis of the psalms, the prophecies, and the historical narratives of Israel. But it is not through nature that man seeks and finds communion with God. It is because God has taken the initiative. He has shown Himself as an understanding, compassionate, and merciful God, ready to forgive.

Unlike the gods of her neighbors, Israel's God is not a complaisant god, permitting rivals. He is jealous and demands her exclusive worship. The history of Israel is the history of her jealous God, Who, as Judge and Savior, intervenes to chastise and to woo her, to heal her to the fulfillment of herself in the Kingdom of the future when Yahweh will instruct all nations in justice and truth. Ineffably mysterious, He is yet present in every phase of history, manifesting His wrath and His favor, His steadfast love and mercy. He is at once "transcendent and immanent and transparent." [1]

[1] John Courtney Murray, "On the Structure of the Problem of God," *Theological Studies* (March, 1962), p. 3.

GOD
IS UNIQUE

✛ ✛ ✛ ✛

CHAPTER ONE

Concerning the complex and vigorously controverted question of monotheism in Israel, there are certain areas of agreement. Although as a matter of historical observation, the ever-recurring worship of strange gods proves that not all Israelites were practising monotheists; yet at the same time, monotheism as a religious tenet is her doctrinal cornerstone.[1] There is general agreement that the sole godhead of Yahweh was a doctrinal truth whose light shone more and more strongly upon the Israelites until in the post-Exilic period strict and absolute monotheism became an everyday reality, the hallmark of even the masses of the Jewish people.

One of the main points upon which scholars disagree, however, is the process by which Israelite monotheism was achieved. Some think that the religion of Israel passed through the various rudimentary stages of animism, polydaemonism, polytheism, and henotheism before evolving into the full splendor of mono-

---

[1] Hermann Schultz, *Old Testament Theology* (Edinburgh: T. & T. Clark, 1898), II, 176.

theism. The fallacy of this theory is that it leans upon a false foundation, a radical misinterpretation of biblical literature.[2] This concept of growth emphasizes the processes of human discovery rather than those of revelation. But both elements are found in biblical literature and neither can be discarded. The living God breaks into the life of a people and, by His acts, performs wonders in their behalf. The people see, they hear, they understand, they obey, and they rebel. An evolution must certainly be acknowledged, but it must be one which takes into account the uniqueness of Israel's religion. No evolutionary process can explain matters which belong to the realm of religious faith. Israel borrowed from many sources, but her uniqueness consisted in the alteration and improvements which she imposed on what she borrowed. Even Wellhausen, the initiator of the evolutionary theory, was forced to admit that he could give no satisfactory answer to the question why Chemosh of Moab never became the god of righteousness and the creator of heaven and earth. It would seem clear, then, that the idea of Yahweh as the unique God is not developed from any polytheistic process but from the Mosaic revelation. In point of fact, what separates Judaism from the other religious systems of antiquity is precisely its insistence on the uniqueness of God.

The classical thesis of liberal criticism was that Israel's religion at the time of Moses was monolatry. She adored Yahweh as the God of Israel—but did not deny that Baal existed as the God of the Canaanites. In this thesis Israel would have realized that Yahweh was the God of the entire universe, but not until she had felt the influence of the prophets, starting around the eighth century B.C. Wellhausen would thus explain the evolution of the religion of Yahweh in Israel as a purely rational development, discounting any divine intervention in favor of an elected people. The whole process which ended in monotheism would be considered immanent, natural, and religious, but

---

[2] John J. Dougherty, "The Origins of Hebrew Religion," *Catholic Biblical Quarterly* (1955), pp. 138-56. Cf. Edward P. Arbez and John P. Weisengoff, "Exegetical Notes on Genesis I:1-2, *Catholic Biblical Quarterly* (1948), pp. 140-50.

independent of all revelation. This thesis seems to us untenable for several reasons.

The Old Testament manifests a way of life which was a radical departure from that of the polytheistic world. (This departure was not however the result of speculative thought, any more than was the analysis of the divine among the polytheists.) The power of Yahweh, the God of Israel, was known because He had chosen this people for Himself. He had humbled Pharaoh and delivered Israel from slavery. He had formed a dispirited people into a nation and given them a law and an inheritance. The Israelite knowledge of God was founded therefore on an historical event, not on an awareness of nature, as was the case in polytheism. The original and basic metaphors through which the divine was apprehended were, by the polytheists, derived from nature. When Israel borrowed these terms from her neighbors, it was her intention to indicate only His power. So great was He that the Israelite acknowledged His Lordship over every phenomenon encountered in his experience. The point where that power was apprehended was the starting place of an entirely different faith from that of the polytheist. For the Israelite the problem of life was seen as an adjustment to the will of God Who had chosen them, not as an integration with the forces of nature.[3]

It is impossible therefore to see how this God of Israel could have been the result of a slow evolution from polytheism. The two faiths rest on entirely different foundations. The religion of Israel appears suddenly in history, breaks radically with the existing religions, and is explainable only in terms of a new creation. G. Wright summarizes this viewpoint as follows:

> The Israelite did not analyze the problem of life over against nature. The latter plays a subordinate role in the faith, except as it is used by God to further His work in society and history. Instead, the problem of life is understood over against the will and purpose of the God Who had chosen one people as the in-

[3] H. H. Rowley, *The Faith of Israel* (London: S.C.M. Press, 1956), p. 71.

strument of His universal, redemptive purpose (e.g., Gen. 12:3). This election of a people was not based upon merit, but upon a mysterious grace; and its reality was confirmed by the great saving acts of this God, particularly as expressed in the redemption from Egyptian bondage and in the gift of an inheritance. Here, then, is an utterly different God from the gods of all natural, cultural and philosophic religion. He is no immanent power in nature nor in the natural process of being and becoming! The nature of His being and His will is revealed in His historical acts. He thus transcends nature and He transcends history; and consequently He destroys the whole basis of pagan religion. No force or power in the world is more characteristic of Him than any other, and it is increasingly understood today that the former identifications in early Israel of a Mountain-god, a Fertility-god and a War-god, from which the "ethical monotheism" of the prophets gradually evolved, are figures of scholarly presupposition and imagination. It is impossible on any empirical grounds to understand how the God of Israel could have evolved out of polytheism. He is unique, *sui generis,* utterly different.[4]

It is true that the popular traditions gathered together in Genesis do ascribe various names to the gods of the Patriarchs. This however need not indicate that the Patriarchs were polytheists, since they might merely represent different aspects of the one God. It does not appear that the God of the Patriarchs is limited in His power to one locale, nor even to one tribe. Moreover, Yahweh is never represented as having a consort. In fact, the Hebrew language does not even have its own word for Goddess. Definitely, Jahweh has neither consort nor special relationship to any of the forces of nature.

Still further, the exclusivism of Yahweh is entirely characteristic of the God of Moses and is not found in any other ancient god. Yahweh demands total submission from His subjects. No argument for the admission of other gods can be drawn from the fact that the God of Israel has a proper name— Yahweh. This is not to distinguish Him from other gods, but

---

[4] G. Ernest Wright, *God Who Acts* (London: S.C.M. Press, Ltd., 1958), p. 21. Distributed in U.S.A. by Allenson's, Naperville, Illinois.

to allow the Hebrew worshipper to know Him, to pay Him cult, to come into closer relationship with Him, for to the Hebrew mind one who lacks a name is almost nonexistent.[5]

However, Israel's exalted idea of God did not realize its full flower immediately, even granted the Mosaic revelation. Moses presented Yahweh to the Israelites under precisely those aspects which were to allow for a progressive purification of the idea of ethical monotheism. Yahweh would be progressively understood by the chosen people as a God whose power extended over all nations—Who was far from being limited, like other semitic gods, to the protection of the one nation He had chosen; Who was, in fact, unique.

Moses was thus the architect of Israel's monotheism or, better, the witness to God's revelation of Himself as the unique God. It was Moses who created the extraordinary, unique union between Yahweh and Israel, the adherence of the Israelite to their new God through all the misfortunes and sorrows of their history. Such an adoption of a new God is not unparalleled in the history of religion, but we know of no other instance where a nation adhered to its god when other gods were worshipped with apparently greater success. The monotheism of Moses was effective in practically excluding the existence of other gods even though their existence is not *explicitly* denied.

With these preliminary remarks we will now turn our attention to the development of monotheism, and its expression through the centuries of Old Testament thought and practice.

Almost all scholars agree on the absolute commitment of Israel to monotheism as a *religious belief* at the time of Moses. It was owing to Moses that Yahwistic worship was established on the "love and trust relationship" that developed after the release of the Israelites from Egypt. Doctrinal monotheism seems to take definite shape at the moment when Moses receives the revelation of a God infinitely superior in power to every

[5] Albert Gelin, *The Key Concepts of the Old Testament*, trans. George Lamb (New York: Sheed & Ward, Inc., 1955), p. 20.

variety of Palestinian god, and one Who has chosen as His own the people of Israel. From this point on, the Jews are a monotheistic people although the existence of other gods is not explicitly denied. Most authors seem to agree that the whole history of Israel, from Moses to the Babylonian Exile, is the history of monotheism's struggle to win full acceptance among the Israelites. Israel's spiritual leaders, such as Moses and the prophets, always possessed this conviction, but Israel as a whole was led to this height only after long and tenacious religious education and countless failures. It is not accidental that the oneness of Israel's God and the exigencies of unqualified love and worship for Him are announced in the same biblical passage (Deut. 6:4-5), but the practical application of the doctrine was quite another matter.

Although Yahweh was recognized as the sole God of Israel, for centuries after Moses some Israelites believed in the existence and power of the multiple gods of other nations. Consequently much stress, up until the time of the later prophets (Isaiah, Jeremiah, Ezekiel, Daniel, and so on), is laid not on the denial of existence to other gods but on the denial of Israel's right to have any other. This was neither polytheism, nor monolatry, the cult of Yahweh alone, but implicit monotheism without an explicit exclusion of the existence of other gods.

One of the factors clarifying the uniqueness of the divine nature was certainly the religious clash between prophetic Yahwism and Canaanite Baalism, the former receiving sharp and clear definition through pressure from the latter. The worship of the multiple gods of ancient Palestine made serious inroads upon the exclusive worship of Yahweh, nature worship having a greater attraction for a primitive, agricultural people than the strict and stern discipline imposed by doctrinal monotheism. Yahweh had been the God of the battles of Israel, and was thus suited to be the head of all the affairs of nomadic life. But once the Israelites traded desert wanderings for a more settled agricultural society, the worship of Yahweh by some

Israelites underwent a change in which it was assimilated to idolatry worship on Canaanite models. Yahweh had not previously been the god of the fields and the vineyards, but now the Jews began to speak of Him as the Baal of Israel and to worship Him as a Baal.[6] Eventually the God of Israel took over certain tasks of the Baals, particularly that of giver of fertility or agricultural abundance. In time of crises it was to Yahweh that the Israelites turned, and not to the Baals, whose power was localized.[7] The Gideon stories in Judges offer clear example that loyalty to Yahweh was acknowledged to be incompatible with Canaanite gods and their accompanying practices. The nationalistic Recabites, especially, demanded the exclusive worship of Yahweh, aware that the desert nomadism of Yahweh and the stable agricultural life of Canaan could never fuse.

All the prophets openly professed a strict monotheism: Samuel and Elijah condemned divination and worship of strange gods. Amos declared that Yahweh was the god of foreigners (Amos 1:3-15), of the world, and of the underground world, and all other gods were lies (Amos 2:4). Hosea fought against Baalism and declared that only Yahweh could bring salvation. None of these prophets, however, proclaimed himself as the *creator* of this idea, but each referred to it as well known to the people. Their demands were rather that the people live up to Israel's ancient belief. Neither Amos (2:1) nor Jeremiah (2:5) ever suggested monotheism as a new conception. It is undeniable, however, that the prophets strengthened, in the popular mind, the idea of Yahweh's universal dominion. They also underscored His moral characteristics, e.g., Yahweh demands a moral service; He exacts fidelity, mercy, justice. They insisted too on the interiority of religion.[8]

---

[6] Henry St. John Hart, *A Foreword to the Old Testament* (London: Adam and Charles Black, Ltd., 1951), p. 41.

[7] Theodorus C. Vriezen, *An Outline of Old Testament Theology* (London: Basil Blackwell & Mott, Ltd., 1958), p. 176.

[8] Robert H. Pfeiffer, *Introduction to the Old Testament*, 2d. ed. (London: Adam and Charles Black, Ltd., 1953), p. 235.

In the speeches of the prophets, ridicule of the Baals and glorification of one Yahweh are constantly recurring themes, even as late as Jeremiah:

> There is none like thee, O LORD!
> Thou art great, and thy name is great
> in might. Who would not reverence thee,
> O King of the nations? For this is thy due,
> and there is none like thee among all the wise
> ones of the nations, and among all their royalties.
> —JEREMIAH 10:6-7

That God is *one,* without division into a number of local and individual manifestations, and that He is the *only* God are taught in the Old Testament. But when it came to the matter of practice, not only the people but the kings, and even Solomon himself, were either devoted to the worship of strange gods or tolerated its practice.

The great commandment of Deuteronomy:

> Listen, O Israel: the LORD is our God,
> the LORD alone; so you must love the LORD
> your God with all your mind and all your
> heart.
> —DEUTERONOMY 6:4-5

seems to belong to the stage when Yahweh alone was recognized as one and as the God of Israel, having fully supplanted the Canaanite Baals.[9] At that point of recognition men needed to be reminded that He was not only Israel's God, but that there was not one Yahweh of Jerusalem, another of Jericho, and so on. In the struggle against the doctrinal inroads of Baalism, all the ancient holy places, except that of Jerusalem, were rejected for the worship of Yahweh Himself. Before the commandment of Deuteronomy, however, a kind of poly-Yahwism had developed that threatened the true ethical unity of Israel's God.

---

[9] W. O. E. Oesterley and Theodore H. Robinson, *An Introduction to the Books of the Old Testament* (London: S.P.C.K. Press, 1955), p. 51.

The history of Israel was the theater for the progressive de-thronement of other gods. At the beginning of the world, Yahweh triumphed over His rivals, and later the affirmation of this victory developed into a denial of their power. As Israel became conscious of herself as a nation, with the struggle of Saul and David against the Philistines, a consciousness of one people under one God arose such as had never existed before.

Later on, in pre-Exilic prophesy, Yahweh came to be explicitly spoken of more and more as the universal God. Notice, for example, the progression manifest in going from these lines of Exodus:

> Who is there like thee among the gods,
> O LORD? Who is there like thee, . . .
> —EXODUS 15:11

to these from Isaiah:

> Remember the former things of old,
> for it is I who am God, and there is
> no other—The God, and there is none like me.
> —ISAIAH 46:9
> I am the first, and I the last;
> Apart from me there is no God.
> —ISAIAH 44:6

and to these from Job:

> Who stretched out the heavens by himself,
> And treads upon the billows of the sea.
> —JOB 9:8

Job and Second Isaiah solidified the work of their predecessors by clearly attributing to Yahweh the creation of the physical world, concluding that no other god could exist by the side of Yahweh whose control embraced both mankind and nature.[10]

This doctrine of the prophets eventually succeeded, and the Psalms and the books of Wisdom all celebrate the unique God, Creator of heaven and earth.

---

[10] Paul van Imschoot, *Théologie de l'ancien testament* (Tournai: Desclée et Cie., 1956), II, 96.

It is unusual that the Old Testament emphasizes the uniqueness of God as a *speculative* truth, Job perhaps being the only notable exception. What is emphasized is that the Lord is really God, but the emphasis is upon the nature of His divinity rather than upon His ontological unity. God as single and unitary was reached through an intuitive and spontaneous act of faith, and His unity was looked upon as a constituent element of His being. Genuine, religious monotheism consists in this, and in trusting the true spiritual God and Him alone. God proved Himself to the Israelites and hence the basis was laid for a monotheism. Rather than through logical analysis, the approach to God was by way of actual religious experience. It was the social experience of Israel, however, and not the reflective experience of the individual Israelite that made up the historical ground for achieving monotheism—the result of prolonged and decisive acquaintance with Yahweh. The Israelite writers accomplished this by reducing to impotence the recurring idols of the day. They were not so much interested in monotheism as an idea as in deepening and extending the influence of God in the lives of the Israelite community. In God alone did they find the means of help; the first result was practical monotheism, belief in a living God Who acts in history. First and foremost, He was a moral God, a righteous God, Who demanded from the Israelites exclusive love and devotion in return for the divine selection of Israel for the redemption of the world.

Several authorities place the advent of a strict and absolute *theoretical* monotheism with Isaiah at a time in history when the Israelites were confronted with a heathen situation. Isaiah is thus said to be the first author to deny categorically the existence of other gods. Some hold that strict monotheism began with Jeremiah, whereas others, who claim for Isaiah this honor, comment that similar denials of monolatry and polytheism were demonstrably later than 500 B.C. For Isaiah, the first Commandment is religiously and psychologically necessary, because of the exclusive demands of love for the Holy One of Israel.

The prophetic mission bore practical fruit in the post-Exilic period. The unity of God as a firmly established doctrine was viewed not only from the religious standpoint, but from the theological and speculative areas as well. Although the older methods of expression were not altogether discarded, the scrupulous monotheism which evolved over centuries caused the Israelites to eliminate the proper name Yahweh. It was a period in which theology outran politics.[11]

The Exile marks a definite division in Israel's religious practice and belief; not only was idolatry no longer practiced by the people and their leaders, but it disappeared completely and forever from the midst of the Hebrew nation.

Approaching the time of Christ, Jewish theology, as reflected in the Wisdom of Solomon, was considerably more monotheistic than other Wisdom literatures. Somewhat later, Tacitus' note on the Jews expressed skepticism at their eternal "one god only." The austere monotheism of the synagogues of the era, however, attracted serious men. For the Jews, theology and religious practice had come a long way from the fertility rites of their Canaanite neighbors.

From the moment that Moses planted in Israel's consciousness the belief that Yahweh was capable of fulfilling Israel's every need, the germ of progressive development was sown. As Israel grew as a nation and came into contact with other nations, the universal dominion of Yahweh could not but be affirmed, gradually but surely. Some Israelites may have and did worship other gods, but they were never allowed to do so with a peaceful conscience. Israel's history and her spiritual leaders spoke out against this practice.[12]

We must distinguish then between what is implicit and what is explicit, and between official Yahwism and popular religion. From Moses on, implicit monotheism was the official

---

[11] John L. McKenzie, *The Two-Edged Sword, An Interpretation of the Old Testament* (Milwaukee: Bruce Publishing Co., 1956), p. 287.
[12] H. Wheeler Robinson, *The Religious Ideas of the Old Testament* (London: Gerald Duckworth & Co., Ltd., 1952), p. 59.

religion of Israel; its theoretical consequences were not thought out completely, but the existence of other gods was in practice excluded in official Yahwism. The people, however, continued to worship other gods until the fifth century before Christ. The prophets purified the popular ideas by a return to Israel's primitive belief and by explicating it; this progressive understanding of Moses' teaching was due, not to any necessary, immanent evolutionary process, but to the providential action of God in Israel's history and His guidance through her prophets.

Clearly, the Old Testament has made a highly significant contribution to the religious thought of the world in its doctrine of ethical monotheism. The Jewish religion of today, Mohammedanism, and Christianity are all its heirs on this point.

GOD
THE HOLY ONE

✠ ✠ ✠ ✠

CHAPTER TWO

The importance of the concept of holiness for the doctrinal development of the Old Testament is difficult to estimate, not because its indications are rare or especially obscure, but because the concept itself has such wide application and is a part of so many other Old Testament ideas. It is so basic a concept that many scholars and exegetes of the Old Testament use it as a heading for the entire doctrine of God, some even extending its primacy into the teaching of the New Testament.[1] Holiness, in its formulation as a Levitical code of law, constitutes perhaps the most conspicuous determining principle of the entire Pentateuch; it is insisted upon emphatically and frequently, and becomes the leading motive of Leviticus. In fact, so systematic is the latter's preoccupation with it that authorities have termed the seventeenth to the twentieth chapters "the Code of Holiness."

Not only the author or compiler of the Holiness Code, but

[1] Paul Heinisch, *Theology of the Old Testament,* trans. William Heidt (Collegeville, Minnesota: Liturgical Press, 1950), p. 66.

also the prophet Ezekiel makes holiness the dominant element in the relations between the Lord and His people of Israel. As the concept develops, it appears more and more the force on which Israel's inner life depends and from which it is renewed. It is the center of the ideas about God and also the basis for the attitudes of the Israelites toward the divine.[2] As a result, it is almost impossible to consider one orientation of holiness without the other. One cannot deal with the idea of "the holy *God*" without considering in some measure its extension to include the *people* whom God had elected and made holy. Nor can one consider God's holiness without at least touching upon the attributes which, in the opinions of most scholars, spring from holiness, such as righteousness, purity, jealousy, and that which is most closely allied to holiness, the *glory* of God.

After a discussion of the origins of the idea of holiness, both etymologically and as a primitive concept, we propose to investigate the concept in its applications to Yahweh and to the chosen people, its growth, and some of the conflict which centered around it at times, such as the supposed discrepancy between the interpretation of holiness according to the prophets and that according to the priests. We will then deal with some of the objections which have been raised, on doctrinal grounds particularly, to the idea of God's holiness and its manifestations. And finally, we will discuss the concept of the *glory* of God.

I

The etymology of the word *holy* as it was used by Semitic peoples and by the Israelites in particular is by no means the least discussed of the problems concerning God's holiness. Some authorities feel that, in the final analysis, the etymology of the

---

[2] Albert Gelin, *The Key Concepts of the Old Testament,* trans. George Lamb (New York: Sheed & Ward, Inc., 1955), p. 29.

word will have to remain uncertain, and that in any case it
makes little difference, since the breadth and depth which the
concept assumes in Old Testament theology go far beyond whatever content the original root might have possessed. Nevertheless, most scholars have quite definite ideas on the origins of
holy as a combined noun-adjective, ideas which in some cases
seem to reflect the prevailing religious attitudes of the individual scholar.

According to some, the word holy is derived from *qadad,*
"to cut off," and thus takes on two aspects: (1) separation and
removal from all things profane and unclean, and (2) appointment to Yahweh's service. Actually, the original etymological
significance of holy might better be expressed by the two English words "holy" and "clean." To become holy a person or
object must become clean, that is, removed from all profane use
and in some fashion dedicated to God.[3]

Other scholars emphasize the aspect of separation, referring
to "the fearful and alluring mystery," and pointing to the
Hebrew concept of God as the wholly Other. Thus they feel
that holiness refers secondarily to God's moral perfection and
primarily to His absolute inaccessibility, His ineffable mysteriousness.[4]

Of itself, holiness in the Old Testament does not necessarily
imply moral perfection, but rather either a mysterious and fearful "presence" in an object or place, or separation from profane
use and dedication to cultic use. It is often attributed in the
Old Testament to times and persons, to places and objects in
this sense of a mysterious force contained in them. Failure to
recognize this holy character of an object or place may result
in death. When the High Priest enters the Holy of Holies, he
is entering a spot charged with the divine presence and the
bells attached to his vestments protect him from death. The
vessels used in the service of the cult are withdrawn from pro-

[3] Walther Eichrodt, *Theology of the Old Testament,* trans. J. A. Baker (Philadelphia: Westminster Press, 1962), I, 271.
[4] *Ibid,* p. 270.

fane use because they are holy and they are not to be touched
by any except the Levites for fear of death. So too, the spot
where Yahweh visits Jacob in a dream is holy, and when Jacob
realizes this, he is filled with terror. The Ark of the Covenant,
the symbol of Yahweh's presence, may not be touched except
by the Levite. The ritual vestments used by the priest in his
sacred functions are also holy and may communicate this holiness to other things which they happen to touch. Something of
this same idea of a mysterious force intrinsic to an object or
person is found in the idea of the miracle worker, who is holy
because he possesses this strange power from God.[5]

At times scholars have attempted to explain this early concept
of holiness as a sort of primitive, magical conception. In this
view holiness would be a quasi-physical quality of nonhuman
origin similar to the *mana* of animistic religions. There would
be an impersonal but superhuman power or force in the object. Anything connected with the gods of the community could
fall under the domination of a strange power, like a taboo. In
this theory any strictly *moral* element would be lacking in the
concept of holiness. The prostitutes of the Canaanite sanctuaries are "holy" in this sense, in that they are separated from
the ordinary sphere of life.

However, in the religion of Israel the central emphasis of
this type of nonmoral holiness appears to be rather the fearful
aspect of that which is in some way not only separated from
profane use but also in connection with Yahweh or the cult of
Yahweh. The basic reason for the extraordinary power inherent
in a place or an object is its relationship to Him Who is holy
above all, and Yahweh, even from the earliest times, is seen as
morally holy.[6]

Certain days, such as the Sabbath, are holy in the sense of
separation from the profane and dedication to Yahweh because

---

[5] Paul van Imschoot, *Théologie de l'ancien testament* (Tournai: Desclée et Cie.,
1954), I, 44.
[6] Theodorus C. Vriezen, *An Outline of Old Testament Theology* (London: Basil
Blackwell & Mott, Ltd., 1958), p. 152.

they are reserved to the cult of Yahweh. God Himself has withdrawn the day from profane use and sanctified it, i.e., dedicated it to His service. His tabernacle is holy because it is His dwelling place. The holy city is holy because it contains the holy temple wherein He dwells. Whatever is offered to God and withdrawn from man's usage shares the holiness of God, to Whom it is dedicated. The showbread is holy, as are the oil used in ritual anointings, the altar and furnishings of the temple, the sacrifices, and whatever is offered to the sanctuary. The priest and all that is connected with the ritual are holy. In the evolution of the concept of holiness this central meaning of appurtenance to the ritual or to Yahweh gradually took prominence over the more primitive idea of a mysterious inner power.[7]

Holiness receives its first declaration during Moses' song of praise (Exod. 15:11) in which God is described as "glorious in holiness." Here holiness is brought into close connection with the covenant and, as such, signifies two things from the start: being taken out of worldliness, and being appropriated by God. Whenever this character of holiness pertains to something or someone, it never rests on merely natural qualities, for the idea of natural purity and impurity does not coincide with that of holiness or unholiness.[8] The holiness of the creature always goes back to an act of the divine will; it is always a state in which the creature is bound to God by the appointment of God Himself. Its holiness is somehow related to God's holiness. His holiness is, from the beginning, His Self-identity, by virtue of which He remains like Himself in all relations which either are in Him or in which He enters in any way; He neither gives up any part of His divinity nor accepts anything ungodly. Two things are here implied: opposition to the world, and removal of this opposition by God's choice in the world of those whom He

[7] van Imschoot, op. cit., 46.
[8] H. H. Rowley, Rediscovery of the Old Testament (Philadelphia: Westminster Press, 1946), p. 190.

places in communion with Himself. Thus, all demonstrations of the divine covenant of grace might be called effects of the divine holiness.

Even in Exodus 15:11, holiness already denotes more than separation from uncleanliness; it implies majesty, greatness, exaltation, matchlessness. Often "holy" appears to sum up all the other perfections of God, suggesting especially His supreme power. "God" and "Holy One" are actually synonymous, although perhaps not expressed as such until fairly late, when, for example, Ezekiel (3:16-22) says that God makes Himself known as Yahweh, the mighty and true God of Israel, by sanctifying Himself or manifesting His holiness. God swears by His holiness as He swears by Himself. It has been noted that since the Hebrews said "holy" where we say "divine" or "heavenly," holiness can denote the entirety of the divine character, and that the best English expression for "holy" would perhaps be "divine exaltation" or "majesty."

It is well to recall, however, that in attempting to grasp the Hebrew attitude toward the majesty of Yahweh we must leave behind as far as possible the spiritual climate of our own times and try to recapture the awe felt by the Hebrews toward the terrifying power of the holy God of Israel.

II

We must now examine the concept of holiness in the Old Testament seen as a whole. Actually the two subjects overlap somewhat, but there are some later developments in doctrine and application which do not appear in an investigation of the earlier ideas of holiness. Holiness in the Pentateuch always connotes omnipresence; beyond this, the Pentateuch has mainly to do with the *special* presence which God gives by living among His people when He localizes His face, His name, His glory.

As remarked above, the more ancient approach of Israel to

God's holiness did accent a numinous and terrifying, yet attractive, aspect rather than the essential moral aspects of holiness.[9] When approached by God man feels his utter lowliness and sinfulness. His first reaction may well be one of fear as was that of Isaiah. Man is separated from God by a distance which only God's initiative can suppress. To recognize God's nearness and His holiness is to fear Him. God is completely different from man. He is the all-powerful, the mysterious, and the terrifying, and before Him man may well tremble with reverence and fear. Moses prepared the people for the descent of Yahweh among them, for they were to experience the presence of one who is fearful in His majesty. The Israelites had to be prepared lest Yahweh would strike them dead. Moses and Elijah hid their faces in dread at the approach of Him, for no one can see God and live (Exod. 33:20). Moses perfectly expresses this sentiment of the numinous:

> Who is there like thee among the gods, O LORD?
> Who is there like thee, so glorious in holiness,
> So awe-inspiring in renown, such a wonder worker?
> Thou didst stretch out thy right hand, the earth
> swallowed them. In thy goodness thou didst lead
> the people whom thou didst redeem; In thy strength
> thou didst guide them to thy holy abode. When the
> nations heard of it, they trembled, Agony seized the
> inhabitants of Philistia; Then were the chieftains
> of Edom dismayed; The lords of Moab—trembling
> seized them; All the inhabitants of Canaan melted
> away. Terror and dread fell upon them;
> —EXODUS 15:11-16

Abraham was seized with terror and felt himself dust and ashes before God; Isaiah almost despaired; Daniel fell to the ground with his face pressed to the earth before Yahweh. Isaiah

---

[9] Eichrodt, *Theology of the Old Testament*, I, 272. Cf. Ludwig Köhler, *Old Testament Theology*, trans. A. S. Todd (Philadelphia: Westminster Press, 1957), pp. 51-53.

declares that the Holy One of Israel will be as a flame and his thorn and his briars shall be set on fire and shall be devoured in one day. Before His majesty the earth trembles. An essential element of Yahweh's holiness then is His power. "Who is able to stand before the LORD, this Holy God?" (I Sam. 6:20). But the power of God and His holiness are particularly revealed in the great deeds that He does for Israel. The work of creation was a work of His holiness, and the work of deliverance of the chosen people was also a work of holiness. Because He has made a covenant with Israel, His holiness impels Him to exert His power in her behalf. All His acts to save Israel testify to His holiness.[10] The very name "Holy One of Israel" demonstrates the close relationship between God's holiness and the covenant. He cannot tolerate that His name be profaned, that His holiness be disregarded. For this reason He punishes the enemies of Israel, manifesting His power by prodigies in Israel's behalf. He is said to "sanctify" His name when He proves His holy power. For the honor of His name, He will restore Israel.

Scholars agree as to the great exaltation of God which took place in the post-Exilic period, involving deeper, more spiritualized concepts and the introduction of intermediate Beings. Some scholars believe that in the post-Exilic period, Yahweh, the intimate and familiar friend of the Patriarchs, becomes the transcendent God with an unspeakable name Who has created the world simply by a series of commands. This later idea of God, however, is far from being a mere metaphysical abstraction. The more physical aspects are, indeed, either abandoned or resolved into conscious imagery. Yet the *psychical* side—the ascription of human thoughts, feelings, and desires to Yahweh—is still largely uncriticized. Nevertheless there is a growing consciousness in the Old Testament of the inadequacy and incon-

---

[10] Edmund Jacob, *Theology of the Old Testament,* trans. A. W. Heathcote and Philip J. Allcock (New York: Harper & Row, Publishers, 1958), p. 89.

gruity of what may be called physical anthropomorphisms; and this consciousness culminates in the post-Exilic emphasis on the divine transcendence, with its complementary idea of angelic mediation between God and man.

Isaiah is instrumental in this development. He raises the idea of the God of Israel to a new majesty of conception by his repeated emphasis on the divine holiness; and Isaiah's conception of holiness is not, as has been claimed, a mere symbol of moral righteousness.

The aspect of transcendence has been emphasized by some who point out that the term "Holy One of Israel" does not mean that God's holiness sprang from His relation to Israel. Unlike some heathen deities, Yahweh was always conceived of as having His own unique essence of holiness. It is also observed that, whatever specific conceptions may later be associated with holiness, Israel never lost the idea that God is unapproachable, numinous, and a Being to be feared. Nor does this contradict the earlier idea of God as the "intimate and familiar" friend of the Patriarchs.

Despite this development it must be underscored that from the beginning Israel's God had been a moral God and the concept of His holiness also included His sinlessness and hatred of sin. Isaiah's call demonstrates this, for his terror is precisely due to God's holiness and his own lowliness and sinfulness. When Isaiah heard the angels chanting "Holy, Holy, Holy," he grasped the fact that God demanded holiness also of him. Holiness is so identified with Yahweh that He swears by His holiness. No one is wholly pure before Him. Men may be called holy because they have been set aside for God's service or because of their inner goodness, but their holiness can never be compared to God's. Eliphaz asked Job, "Can a mortal be righteous before God, or a man be pure before his maker?" Between the holiness of the angels and God's holiness there is no comparison (Job 4:17-19). God, unlike His creatures, is above all moral evil; He is without sin and, furthermore, is unable to sin. Israel's entire ethics was founded upon an imitation of this divine holiness.

"You must be holy, for I, the LORD your God, am holy" (Lev. 19:2). And because He is holy, Yahweh hates sin.[11]

We should note too that this ethical holiness of God is not an invention of the prophets, who altered the concept from a magical or numinous one to an ethical one. Moses hides his face from God in Exodus 3:6 because he is a *sinner*. In Genesis God punishes Adam for his transgression, and Cain and the Sodomites are punished because of sin. What the prophets did was to insist upon the inner nature of holiness and to denounce a holiness that would be purely formalistic or ritualistic.

Because Yahweh was holy, he did not permit sin to go unpunished. Israel is called to be holy, and the holiness involved both obedience to ritual precepts and moral precepts. The holiness demanded of Israel in the Old Testament has a personal and moral character quite unique among ancient religions. Israel, however, did not live up to Yahweh's commands, and His punishment fell upon her. Joshua reminded the people that God would not permit disobedience. His holiness was manifest in His judgment of the nations, and also in Israel's misfortunes.

It must also be noted that Yahweh's holiness designates also His condescending grace, self-abasing love, and communication of Himself, and not merely apartness from the creature. In support of this statement one might cite such passages as Psalm 103:1 to demonstrate that holiness was connected with mercy. It has at times been objected that this conception does not really do full justice to biblical thought, and it certainly cannot be denied that the Hebrew expressed awe and fear before the severity and fearfulness of the divinity. The Alexandrian translators were correct in using the word *agios,* since this points to the reverential dread which the Holy demands for Itself. Yet there is some truth to the contentions that holiness contains both transcendence and self-disclosure, for God elects a holy people and does not remain in Himself. One might express this by saying that God's holiness is the interpenetration of His

[11] Heinisch, *Theology of the Old Testament,* p. 67.

transcendence and His self-disclosure, as in Isaiah 57:15. All manifestations of the divine covenant of grace are the issues of the divine holiness. And as soon as the world comes into connection with the divine kingdom, it receives manifestations of the divine holiness. In other words, holiness is not only transcendence; it also permits God's entrance into mysterious relations with man, involving the revelation and communication of Himself.

When compared to God, even the most saintly of men are deficient: "Nor are the stars bright in his eyes" (Job 25:5). And yet even the earliest books of the Bible also imply a nearness of God to man. A notion of God's paternity existed, and it influenced even the naming of Israelite children, such as Abiezer, meaning "My Father is help."

Holiness is the ground for Yahweh's redemptive action in the historical scene. It is both an activating principle in the Old Testament and a principle implying a reality beyond history and the human scene. Holiness is made known for redemptive purposes and, as in Isaiah's case, provides genuine self-knowledge based upon God's own nature and will. Isaiah's vision resulted in contrition and a revelation to him of previously unrealized resources. A God who was but a projection of highly regarded social values could never have provoked such an ethical reaction. He had to be *holy,* and thus truly God, so Isaiah (6:8) could say, "Here am I; send me!"

The holiness of which Israel is the beneficiary can turn against her, and, in certain circumstances in the course of history, the divine holiness was for Israel an effective manifestation of judgment. But the term Holy One of Israel means above all else that Yahweh keeps close to Israel, that He cannot abandon her without denying Himself. Although holiness qualifies God as God, it is also that in Him which is most "human." Thus God "comes down" to the contrite and humble; He is the near relative Who exercises the right of redemption. His relationship to Israel is intimate to the point of jealousy; and, as a matter of fact, holiness and jealousy are both contained in the name Yahweh.

The entire history of Israel can be called the work of God's holiness. But while subordinating holiness to the covenant, Yahweh remains free to manifest His holiness outside the covenant. The possible breaking of the covenant by men does no injury to the divine holiness, because that holiness maintains its extra-covenantal aspect of transcendence. God is holy—and that is one reason why He chooses to enter into the covenant. Man, on the other hand, can become holy only by entering into the covenant.

In a general way, the people in their entirety are the recipients of the holiness of Yahweh; but within the nation there are individuals and objects which are charged more than others with this divine holiness. This "materialization" of holiness could not exist without introducing a great danger which Israel was not always able to resist. Holiness risked being looked upon as linked in a permanent way with certain objects and causing the essential aspect of relationship to Yahweh to be forgotten. In this way the holiness of the Temple, and later that of the law, was seen to take on almost the appearance of idolatry.

In tracing this later development of the concept of holiness, scholars lay stress upon two aspects: (1) a reappearance of the notion of holiness as almost physically connected with an object, a notion which had been supplanted by that of relationship to Yahweh, and (2) the distinction between the sacred and secular worlds found among all those in Judaism who are the heirs of the thought of Ezekiel. Within the sphere of the sacred itself there are various degrees of holiness; there is a distinction between what is holy and what is very holy which would have no meaning if holiness were regarded strictly as a relationship. In addition to this, the "materialization of holiness" led to its being regarded less as an attribute than as a *state,* and to its subsequent identification with ritual *purity.*

The sixteenth chapter of Numbers is the story of a dispute

over degrees of holiness. In this section Korah and those he led
challenge Moses and Aaron: "Enough from you! The whole
community, all of them, are holy; the Lord is in their midst.
Why then should you set yourselves over the Lord's congrega-
tion?" Decision is finally given in favor of a specifically sacer-
dotal kind of holiness; only men detached from the sphere of
the secular and consecrated by special rites can approach God.
On this basis purity becomes the principal content of holiness,
in morals and in ritual, usually both at once. Holiness implies
man's cultic duties as well as his personal attitudes. In this setting, however, emphasis is placed less upon separation than
upon the necessity for man to realize the fullness of his life,
which he will not do without a struggle against the destructive
powers opposed to the fulfillment of his vocation.

The relationship of all holiness with Yahweh makes one
very sceptical about attempts to classify holiness. Yet such attempts have been made. One approach is to regard holiness
chiefly from the viewpoint of distance, distinguishing the following five aspects: (1) inaccessible holiness, (2) holiness of
majesty, (3) holiness of jealousy, (4) holiness of perfection, and
(5) holiness of transcendence.[12] Another, a sociological classification, seems more subtle in its divisions, and therefore is more
preferable: (1) In popular circles holiness evolved from the simple taboo to become the expression of the covenant; (2) Priestly
circles regarded holiness as the setting apart of priests for the
correct approach to sacred things; (3) In the literary prophets
God is holy toward men and holy in Himself.[13]

This attempt at classification of holiness introduces us to the
conflict between the priests and the prophets over the idea of
holiness. The most plausible resolution seems to lie in rejecting
the misleading approach which deals with the supposed moral-
ization of the holiness concept, and which distinguishes strongly

---

[12] J. Haenel, *Die Religion der Heiligheit* (Gütersloh: 1931), cited by Jacob, *op.
cit.*, p. 92 (see footnote).
[13] F. J. Leenhardt, *La Notion de sainteté dans l'ancien testament* (Paris: 1929),
cited by Jacob, *op. cit.*, p. 93 (see footnote).

between *ritualistic* and *ethical* holiness. For both priests and prophets, in effect, interpreted holiness in fundamentally the same way. The viewpoint of the priests is that the community is holy because of its intimate association with its Holy God. God's separateness and uniqueness through holiness pass to the community, and are preserved in the community by the requirements of ritual. Ritual is essentially ethical, but also ensures the preservation of a withdrawn sacred community through the observance of divinely authorized regulations and laws. The prophetic viewpoint also looks on holiness as identifying the ultimate and essential nature of God. The preservation of the community and the fulfillment of its destiny are based on loyalty and knowledge. Man obeys God's will not only because he finds it righteous, but because it is *His* will, the will of the Holy One. God Himself was the source of light and hope, not just particular statutes emanating from Him in the form either of ethical or of ritualistic demands. Thus, in their estimation of the importance of holiness and in their desire to preserve the community, the priests and the prophets are much alike. Both groups are concerned with the glorification of the Holy God by creating a holy community. This holy community is partly for the purpose of glorifying God's name and God's holiness outside the nation of Israel. The conquest of Gentile nations by the Israelites was designed by Yahweh partially as a means for bringing the Gentiles to recognize and acknowledge His power and holiness.

It has sometimes been objected against God's holiness that He showed favoritism by espousing the cause of the Patriarchs and of Israel in every circumstance, even where their actions were ethically wrong. But we must remember that any protection given to the Patriarchs was not for their own personal interest, but for the good of mankind. And obligations to God had always to correspond to privileges; for Israel's rights and privileges had corresponding duties, and God punished when His ordinances were disregarded. Yahweh demanded atonement for sin.

It is also occasionally charged that Yahweh acted capriciously, for example in His killing of the men of Bethshamesh, or in striking down Uzzah when he tried to steady the Ark. But the Bethshameshites were engaging in disrespectful gazing on the holy object, lacking reverence, and Uzzah had no right to touch the Ark since he was not a Levite. Levites should have been there to hold it. God sent this punishment to recall to Israel His demands that cult prescriptions be observed. We should recall too that ancient culture did not possess our sharp distinction between formal and material sin. Cult offenses were often regarded as punishable by death.

Perhaps a more important accusation sometimes leveled against Old Testament holiness is the fact that God seems to manifest traits which are demonic and amoral both from a religious and a theological point of view. In point of fact, however, there is nothing demonic in Yahweh because He is always regarded as a Person, and the demonic always has something infra-personal, something neutral. There are, after all, certain features of God's holiness in the Old Testament which we appreciate less easily, because in many modern conceptions of holiness the moral element has become all-absorbing. The idea of a holy object, a concrete thing charged with God's power and reserved to His service, is no longer familiar to much modern thought.

In the last analysis, all our expressions, all our conceptual formulations are, with regard to the Old Testament, somewhat deficient. They lack the all-important element of contemporaneity, the intimate knowledge of the Hebrew religious consciousness which would dissolve many of the charges and arguments centering upon the Old Testament conception of the divine holiness.

III

Of all the attributes of God in the Old Testament which ultimately spring from the idea of holiness, the most closely allied is the concept of divine glory. According to most scholars, the glory of Yahweh was the outward manifestation of His holiness. There are, it appears, two different representations of glory in the Old Testament: Isaiah saw glory in the power and might manifested in nature and history; Ezekiel, on the other hand, represented it as a physical phenomenon, a bright or fiery appearance indicative of the divine presence. The same view appears in the Priestly Code, with this difference; in Ezekiel, the glory appears only in prophetic visions, while in the Code it manifests itself to ordinary human sight.[14]

Glory might be called what man may know of God. It is the side of divinity accessible to man; the holiness of God is His hidden glory, and the glory of God is His revealed holiness. Holiness is inaccessible transcendence, glory its visible manifestation in the world. Glory expressed itself to the Israelite imagination in terms of fire and light. The appearance of God as consuming fire is the reason why death was feared as a consequence of approaching Him or seeing His face; since He appeared as dazzling light, no one dared look upon His face.

All manifestations of the divine activity in history and in nature, in His judgments and in His benefits, may be regarded as manifestations of His glory. The divine glory reaches beyond the spheres in which the divine holiness operates, for God's glory extends over nature and is attributed to Him by all His creatures. On the other hand, the course of nature serves the divine *holiness* only so far as God employs it for the purposes of His kingdom and makes use of the powers of nature. Thus the indefinite expression "glory" may comprehend both "name" and "countenance," by means of which God can be brought within the immediate knowledge of man.

The link between holiness and glory is also seen in the terms *qodesh* and *kabod*. *Kabod*, the radiant power of God's Being, has aspects of both saving and destruction in its original meaning. It is the terrible splendor underlying *qodesh*: God's

[14] Jacob, *op. cit.*, pp. 79-80.

holiness is the absolute glory of His Being. The root *kbd* probably signifies *weightiness; kabod,* therefore, designated whatever had weight—such as riches, success, beauty—thus inspiring respect and honor. *Kabod* not only points to the obvious objective reality but also to the feeling which is experienced toward that which inspires respect. This double meaning is particularly evoked where God is concerned; God reveals His glory, but His creatures must also give glory unto Him. God possesses glory in His own right—a kind of qualitative totality which sums up His divine power, an incandescent emanation of God's invisible spirit. *Kabod* is always concrete. It is intended to be seen, and so appears generally as light. Exodus 33:18 ff. pictures it as a luminous reality, less directly divine than the face, but still able to annihilate the direct observer, and having a perceptible after-reflection. The Priestly Code sees it as a manifestation of the divine presence. It has probably a multiple origin, both in natural phenomena and in cultic symbols; for example the perpetual lamp in the sanctuary of the Temple.[15]

The concept of glory is extremely important in the writings of Ezekiel. For him *kabod* is not merely the manifestation of God in concrete form; it is *identical* with Him, as in Ezekiel 9, where *kabod* and God are interchangeable. Thus, the prophet insisted that God cannot be seen in His essence, but only in His image. *Kabod* is closely linked with the Temple, as something of a consecration; this linking is not automatic, but due to the free choice of Yahweh. *Kabod* has, in addition, all the mobility of a God Who acts in history to direct history.

There is another difference between Ezekiel and the Priestly Code with regard to glory. For Ezekiel the glory was a permanent presence intended to express the freedom of Yahweh, master of the world and of history; the Code wishes rather to bring to light the reality of Yahweh's approach, whether for salvation or, more often, to announce the punishment of those who have rebelled against His will. But this difference is not

---

[15] Eichrodt, *Theology of the Old Testament,* I, 277.

irreducible. According to Israelite belief, God's glory would one day rise up for all peoples, and Israel saw the preliminary signs of this in the cult and in prophecy.

If there is, after all, any sharp difference between *kabod* and holiness, we may perhaps see it in the fact that *kabod* has sometimes a negative aspect, as a power which overwhelms, and is sometimes connected with terrifying manifestations in nature; holiness, on the other hand, is a life-giving power.

GOD
IS JUST

✠ ✠ ✠ ✠

CHAPTER THREE

The Hebrew terms for justice or righteousness, *sedeq* and *seda-qah,* respectively, accent the general notion of conformity to a rule or norm. Regrettably, the original meaning of the root is lost, but as far as we can determine from Old Testament usage, the fundamental idea is conformity to a standard or norm which requires specific definition in each particular case. Thus, for example, objects are just if they conform to what is expected of them by custom: a balance is just if it is what it should be, a weight is just if it is what it should be, a path is just if it fits our requirements for paths. Since the Hebrew mind does not have an abstract, formal concept which might help to give us a universal norm for justice, we have to look at each situation in the concrete.[1]

When applied to men, justice implies that man conforms himself to what his nature requires; he acts according to accepted social norms and fulfills the duties which arise from his

[1] Jacques Guillet, *Themes of the Bible* (South Bend: Fides Publishers, 1960), p. 25.

social relations with others. Justice in men is fashioned upon
the normal everyday relationships which men have with one another; it is much more an action than a state. When a man
accomplishes all the obligations arising from his relations to God
and to men, he is acting justly. The word often has a contrac-
tual, even forensic, overtone, but it is not exclusively restricted
to this legal sense. The rights and duties of each man arise out
of his particular situation and, consequently, are different according to the relationship he has to others. The justice of a
king is determined by his situation; the justice of a prostitute
by hers. The noblest activity of a ruler is to ensure the protection of law and justice, but, again, justice is not to be thought
of exclusively in terms of law because the word has also, especially when used of God, strong overtones of salvific mercy. At
times the word justice is also used in a broader sense; the man
who is thoroughly virtuous is simply called just, while the sinner is unjust.[2]

When we call Yahweh just, we mean that He exercises somewhat the same conformity to right standards that we expect
from men. In the case of Yahweh, the standard, of course, is His
own Being. But more than this, Yahweh manifests His justice
in maintaining fidelity to the covenant and in His forgiveness
of sins. Hence God's *hesed* (faithfulness) is also a manifestation
of His justice, or at least these two attributes of God explain
one another. God's fidelity is His justice as revealed in the
marvelous fulfillment of His commitment to Israel. God is just
since He always acts according to His own nature, the foundation of justice, and according to the covenant-love He has for
Israel. He does precisely what we should expect from Him: He
judges and saves.[3]

The righteousness of the God of Israel has a fuller meaning
than that of distributive justice, for even where it seems bent

---

[2] Paul van Imschoot, *Théologie de l'ancien testament* (Tournai: Desclée et Cie.,
1954), I, 71.
[3] Walther Eichrodt, *Theology of the Old Testament*, trans. J. A. Baker (Philadelphia: Westminster Press, 1962), I, 241.

on punishment, it remains educative and salvific. His moral will
stands over men, determined upon its own accomplishment and
the fulfillment of Israel; to this task Yahweh bends history and
men, distributing punishment or blessings accordingly as men
fulfill His demands or oppose Him. He renders to each his due.
Since He stands in a covenant relationship to Israel, He is
bound to save her, but in accomplishing this purpose He does
not spare the rod. His justice is exercised within this framework
of the covenant.

Because He is just, Yahweh cannot tolerate sin. He is not
influenced by a person's social or economic situation but tests
the hearts and the reins of kings as well as those of the poor. He
blesses the virtuous and watches over the hearts of men as well
as their exterior beings:

> Be circumcised in heart, then, and do not be stiff-
> necked any more; for the LORD your God is the God
> of gods, and the Lord of lords, the great, mighty
> and awful God, who is never partial, and never
> takes a bribe, who secures justice for the orphan
> and widow, and loves the resident alien in giving
> him food and clothing.
> —DEUTERONOMY 10:16-18

The man who structures his life on Yahweh's will may call upon
Him with confidence:

> O LORD, lead me in thy righteousness, because of
> my enemies; Make thy way straight before me.
> —PSALM 5:8
> How happy is the man to whom the LORD charges
> no guilt, and in whose spirit there is no guile!
> —PSALM 31:2

He is an equitable judge, maintaining right order in the universe and always acting as befits His nature. History is the scene
in which one sees enacted His just judgments. His *sedeq* will
there be made manifest according to the demands of each situation. In the government of the world He always does what fully
suits His aim, and, as a result, He is the stable foundation of

international order and of the order of the universe itself—the
rock of truth upon Whom one may safely lean. Having initiated
a contract with Israel, He is faithful to it even when she is not,
and the guarantee of His merciful kindness and steadfast love
is His justice. Neither will He tolerate strange gods before Him,
nor will He freely absolve the sinner:

> Happy the righteous! for well shall they fare;
> For the fruit of their deeds they shall eat.
> Woe to the wicked! ill shall they fare;
> For the work of their hands shall be paid
> back to them.
>   —ISAIAH 3:10-11

He rebuked Israel severely when she wandered after strange
gods and provoked His anger; yet He will eventually bring her
to salvation for He is a righteous God Who seeks the conversion
rather than the death of the sinner.[4]

Some authorities believe that the idea of Yahweh as a just
God underwent considerable evolution in Israel. Originally,
they maintain, the idea of God's justice had little or no religious
or moral connotation. This moral connotation would have been
introduced by the prophets. Actually, however, Israel's earliest
traditions ascribe a moral justice to Yahweh. Adam and Eve
were punished for their lack of submission to His will; mankind was punished for its faults by the flood; Sodom and
Gomorrah perished in flames for their crimes. Yahweh was willing to save Noah because Noah was just. Reuben said to his
brothers that they would have to expiate the crime they had com-
mitted against Joseph; David accepted Nathan's rebukes and
threats, because he was aware that Yahweh was just. Abraham
did not accept the proposition that Yahweh would destroy the
just and the unjust alike. Thus, the God of the Hebrews was
just from the beginning. He is a holy God Who commits no
moral fault Himself; He is a just God Who punishes the

---

[4] Paul Heinisch, *Theology of the Old Testament,* trans. William Heidt (Collegeville, Minnesota: Liturgical Press, 1955), p. 89.

wicked. He is just in that He overwhelms the just man with
peace and abundance.

From the Semitic ambience of the Old Testament one would
normally expect that the idea of God's justice would occur early
in Israel's thinking. Among the Semites the god of the tribe
was ordinarily regarded as a judge, and in Israel the idea of
justice never lost this fundamental connection with the judicial
process. The tribal chief was the normal representative of god in
preserving law and equity. The Babylonians, the Canaanites,
and the Hebrews all possessed from earliest times this concept
of their god as the defender of equity and law. Like the head
of a tribe, Yahweh would resolve the disputes between Israel
and her neighbors and between individual Israelites in a just
and impartial manner. Israel also used a great many proper
names which indicate that Yahweh was considered a just Judge.[5]

Since Yahweh has concluded an alliance with Israel, He has,
by this gracious act, established Himself as her special protector.
But He also demands that she fulfill her side of the contract,
and not infrequently the covenant is expressed in the figure of
a lawsuit: God initiates legal process against His unfaithful
partner. His judgment will be just and Israel must submit. Still
this justice is not purely forensic. It is always conformable to His
salvific purpose, which is to bring Israel to the Kingdom promised to her ancestors. Yahweh can bring Israel victory by anger,
threats, and by defeating the armies who oppose her:

> If a man sin against his neighbor, and an oath be
> laid upon him compelling him to swear, and he come
> and swear before thine altar in this house, then
> hear thou in the heavens; take action and judge thy
> servants, punishing the wicked by bringing his course
> of action upon his own head, and vindicating the
> righteous by rewarding him according to his righteousness.
> —I KINGS 8:31-32

[5] Edmund Jacob, *Theology of the Old Testament*, trans. A. W. Heathcote and
Philip J. Allcock (New York: Harper & Row, Publishers, 1958), p. 97.

Isaiah demonstrated with what terrible severity the justice of Yahweh can fall upon the enemies of Israel, but he also evolved the idea that Yahweh not only judges, but He *justifies*, and His justice is made manifest in the forgiving of the sinner. The full realization of God's justice comes about when, at the tribunal of justice, He accepts man's deficient and partial justice and declares him just.

Justice should also be characteristic of those who officially represent God upon earth: the king, the priest, and the prophet. Since equity and discernment were among the prime requisites for those who were to rule in God's name, Solomon asked Yahweh for wisdom in judgment, and the first rulers of Israel were called judges. In the earlier period of the Old Testament, the justice of God was regarded primarily in terms of His covenant obligation to protect His elected people. He assured victory in war and so demonstrated His justice. Later, however, the idea of His justice becomes more universal. He is seen as the foundation of international and cosmic order; as the Lord of History he uses events and personalities to chastise as well as to bless.

The Law given on Sinai was the expression of God's just will, and all administration of justice in Israel rested upon this revealed foundation, which had Yahweh as its protector and avenger. His demands that this Law be fulfilled brought home to the popular mind the idea of His own inflexible righteousness and freedom from the arbitrary.

At times it has been objected that Yahweh seems to act arbitrarily. Does He not, after all, favor the Patriarchs and Israel in rather partial fashion? However, one must recall that His protection of Israel does not infringe the rights of other nations. Nor is Yahweh the capricious or amoral God he might seem to be from a superficial reading of some Old Testament stories. He did not approve of the lie of Abraham in passing his wife off as his sister (Gen. 12:18; 20:9), and Jacob's tricks were punished by exile and suffering. When the Old Testament writers

put on Yahweh's lips the command to totally destroy captives
and conquered cities, we must recall that Israel believed she was
engaged in a total war on the enemies of Yahweh and that Old
Testament writers regularly ascribed to Yahweh the actions of
secondary causes. *Herem,* the destruction of men, women, children, and cattle, is not an ethically admirable practice. However we should recall here that Israel's conduct in war was less
severe than her neighbors, and that the moral education of a
people does not take place overnight.

The justice of Yahweh need never be divorced from His
salvific action. Grace, liberality, and forgiveness always under-
lay the concept. It is noteworthy that the prophet Hosea, when
speaking of the gifts he made to his unfaithful wife on her return, chose precisely these words, justice and judgment, to indicate his loving attitude toward her. In the Psalms, in Isaiah,
in Hosea, and in Daniel justice often occurs in connection with
the idea of deliverance, mercy, fidelity to the covenant, and the
promises attached to it. God accomplishes the salvation of Israel
by means of His constant love or His justice, or both. He ensures that Israel and the individual Israelite turn to Him and,
freely changing from indocile to docile, be made just by God.
From the time of Jeremiah the Old Testament accents more and
more strongly this salvific content of God's justice. The terrible
sufferings Israel underwent in the Exile were understood to
have been sufficient punishment for her, and henceforth God's
justice was aimed at her redemption through His gracious
mercy. In the books of Deuteronomy and Isaiah, especially, justice has become synonymous with grace and redemption, for the
faithful Israelite will see the salvation of her people in the Kingdom of Yahweh. The covenant will extend to all the nations
who will seek instruction and find justice at Zion.[6]

It is perceived in Deutero-Isaiah that Yahweh will exercise His
redemptive activity to restore His covenanted people, drawing
them and also the Gentiles to a new state of internal righteous-

---

[6] Eichrodt, *Theology of the Old Testament,* I, 245-48.

ness in imitation of His own justice. The nation of Israel and all nations will order civic and private life so as to reflect Yahweh's justice, and in turn He will bless them with prosperity. The meaning of Yahweh's creative activity will be fully revealed in the consummation of the world when all men will share in the covenant. Whereas in earlier days men invoked the divine justice to punish the heathen and protect the people of the covenant, in Deutero-Isaiah Yahweh's saving righteousness extends to the universe as a whole. God's justice is seen as a personal attribute that transcends the idea of retributive justice and implies a fellowship with all creatures. His justice will restore Israel morally, render her conformed to His will, and then extend its saving action to all creation. The punishments He visits on the world will purify Israel and the nations and assure social and individual integrity. Earth and mankind will be transformed. The desert will become an orchard and the orchard a forest; right will reign where the desert lands were, justice will reign in the city, and peace will mark the accomplishment of Yahweh's justice.

THE
GOD
OF THE
COVENANT

✛ ✛ ✛

CHAPTER FOUR

Fundamental to Israel's religion is the idea of the covenant:
that Yahweh has bound Himself to Israel by a free choice, forging a bond between Himself and the chosen people which marks
them out for a special destiny. Israel thus belongs to Yahweh
and is different from all other peoples. By a pure grace on the
part of God, she has been selected for a mission which implies
mutual but unequal responsibilities and obligations: she will
be Yahweh's people and He will be her God.

Since this idea is paramount throughout the Old Testament,
summing up as it does the special relationship between God and
the Hebrew people, it is important to understand the nature of
the bond, its implications, and its relationship to the rest of Old
Testament theology. In addition, one must consider the problem of whether there were several covenants or whether only
one is continually being referred to.

Until recently the covenant between Yahweh and Israel had
been regarded as modeled on modern Arabian Bedouin clan
treaties which were essentially agreements among equals to
establish order and peace in nomadic society, binding both par-

ties to the same stipulations. In a brief article in 1954, however, G. E. Mendenhall showed that the Sinai covenant is based on the concept of an international treaty of a sovereign with his subject which prevailed in Western Asia during the second millennium before Christ.[1] Instead of being an agreement among equals, it is a pact between a sovereign authority and lesser rulers or kings, who bind themselves by oath to obey the commands of the suzerain. The covenant between God and Israel is clearly not between equals, for Yahweh is the Great King Who claims the obedience of all earthly rulers.

The fundamental elements of the international treaties on which Israel's covenant with God is modeled are six. There is, first of all, a preamble which identifies the Great King Who initiates the covenant by His gracious liberality and which gives His titles and attributes:

> God spoke all these words, saying, "Since I, the Lord
> am your God, who brought you out of the land of Egypt,
> out of a state of slavery. . . ."
> —EXODUS 20:1-2

There follows the second element, an historical prologue, which describes the gracious acts of the King with regard to His subjects, stimulating gratitude and affection among them as they become conscious of His fidelity and their salvation. In the Old Testament the classic example of Yahweh's benevolent acts is, of course, the Exodus. Joshua describes them as follows:

> . . . . When they had presented themselves before God,
> Joshua said to all the people, "Thus says the Lord, the God
> of Israel: 'In days of old your fathers lived beyond the
> River, namely Terah, the father of Abraham and Nahor,
> and served alien gods; but I took your father Abraham from
> beyond the River, and I had him range the whole land of
> Canaan, and made his descendants numerous. I gave him
> Isaac, and to Isaac I gave Jacob and Esau. I gave the

---

[1] G. E. Mendenhall, "Covenant Forms in Israelite Tradition," *Biblical Archeologist*, XVII, No. 3 (September, 1954), 26-46, 50-76. Cf. K. Baltzer, *Das Bundesformular* (Neukirchen, Austria: Kreis Moers, 1960).

highlands of Seir to Esau to occupy, whereas Jacob and his
children went down to Egypt. Then I sent Moses and
Aaron, and I smote Egypt with what I did in her midst.
After that I brought you out; I brought your fathers out
of Egypt, and when you reached the sea, the
Egyptians pursued your fathers with chariotry and
cavalry to the Red Sea; but when they cried to the
Lord, he put darkness between you and the Egyptians,
and brought the sea over them, and engulfed them.
You saw with your own eyes what I did in Egypt.
You lived for a long time in the desert, and then I
brought you to the land of the Amorites who lived beyond
the Jordan. They fought with you, but I delivered them
into your power, so that you took up possession of their
land since I exterminated them from your way. Then
Balak, the son of Zippor, king of Moab, appeared, and
fought against Israel. He sent for Balaam, the son of
Beor, to curse you; but I would not listen to Balaam,
so he had to bless you, and thus I saved you from his
power. Crossing the Jordan, you arrived at Jericho,
and the citizens of Jericho fought against you, as well
as the Amorites, Perizzites, Canaanites, Hittites,
Girgashites, Hivvites, and Jebusites; but I delivered
them into your power. I sent leprosy ahead of you to
drive the two Amorite kings out of your way; it was not
done by your sword nor your bow. I gave you a land on
which you had never labored, and cities in which you
settled without having built them, vineyards and olive
groves from which you eat without having planted them.' "

—JOSHUA 24:2-13

Recalling this generosity on the part of Yahweh, the people
should be more ready to accept the obligations resulting from
the covenant.

The third element enumerates the obligations of the subject
kings, stipulates that foreign alliances are forbidden, prohibits
plots against the sovereign, and so on. In Israel the first commandment forbids any entanglements with foreign deities:

You must have no other gods beside me.

—EXODUS 20:3

> Therefore, stand in awe of the Lord, and serve him faith-
> fully and loyally; remove the gods whom your fathers served
> beyond the River, and in Egypt, and serve the Lord.
> —JOSHUA 24:14

The Great King does not interfere in the internal civil or daily
life of the subject kingdom which remains governed by a vassal
king. However, religious obligations in Israel are stipulated by
the Decalogue and later, especially after the seventh century,
by the written law, which is used to enforce morality.

The fourth stipulation in the typical suzerainty treaty is that
the covenant must be written down, or otherwise it is completely inoperative. It is then deposited in the sanctuary of the
vassal and read to the people at regular intervals. Similar pro-
visions in Israel are narrated in Joshua:

> So Joshua made a covenant with the people that day; he
> made statutes and Joshua wrote these regulations in the book
> of the law of God; and taking a large stone, he set it up
> there under the oak that was in the sanctuary of the Lord.
> Then Joshua said to all the people, "See, this stone
> shall be a witness against us; for it has heard all the words
> that the Lord has said to us; so it shall be a witness
> against you, lest you deny your God."
> —JOSHUA 24:25-27

and in Deuteronomy:

> When Moses had written this code, he committed it to the
> priests, the descendants of Levi, who carried the ark of the
> covenant of the Lord, and to all the elders of Israel.
> Then Moses commanded them as follows: "At the end of
> every seven years, in the time of the year of remission,
> at the feast of booths, when all Israel comes to visit the
> Lord your God at the sanctuary which he chooses, you must
> read this code in the hearing of all Israel, assembling the
> people, men, women, and children, and any aliens in your
> employ that are in your community, that they may hear it,
> and learn to stand in awe of the Lord your God, and be
> careful to observe all the provisions of this code;
> and that their children who do not know it may hear it,
> and learn to stand in awe of the Lord your God; as long

as you live upon the land into which you are crossing
the Jordan for conquest."

—DEUTERONOMY 31:9-13

Thus, the Decalogue of the Old Testament was kept in the Ark
of the Covenant which reposed in the sanctuary when conditions
allowed.

The fifth element was the invoking of the gods as witnesses.
In Israel this element was quite naturally missing, but it is
described in Joshua how the people are called upon to witness:

> So Joshua said to the people, "You are
> witnesses against yourselves that you
> have chosen the Lord as the one to serve."
> "We are witnesses," they said.
>
> —JOSHUA 24:22

Blessings for those who keep the covenant and curses for
those who violate it are the final element in this type of suzerain
treaty. Exodus 23:20-33, Leviticus 26, Deuteronomy 27-28 con-
tain such formulae.

When authority passed from hand to hand it was done during the lifetime of the one originally possessing it. This was
because a suzerainty treaty had its force only during the lifetime
of the vassal. If the chain of succession were to be broken it
would be catastrophic. The covenant renewals practiced in
Israel may be due to this fact or to the calamities which befell
the nation when it was unfaithful to the stipulation of the
covenant (Exodus 34; Nehemiah 9-10; Jeremiah 34:8-22). When
the covenant had been broken by sin, it was renewed in much
the same form as the original treaty. Hence, in Israel, the
people were able to understand life as fidelity to the moral will
of Yahweh, within a covenant framework borrowed from the
suzerainty treaty of the second millennium before Christ. The
covenant thus pervades the whole religious life of Israel, unifying and stabilizing it. It was, in fact, regarded as the most solemn
form of spoken word, the most binding of obligations.

The covenant between men established a kind of artificial
kinship. Since a kinsman was bound to protect the life, goods,

and name of his kin, no matter how great the personal cost, and the survival of the group itself depended upon the covenant fidelity of the kinsmen, the covenant was more than a contract: it was an integral part of the social life.[2]

Since the essence of the covenant was that the contracting parties be present, the Hebrew tradition described the Lord as manifesting Himself in "smoke and flame" at Sinai. Although it has not been ascertained with certainty precisely what kind of convulsion is described in the book of Exodus, there is no doubt that some kind of convulsion took place. The covenant rests on the belief that the Hebrews at Sinai experienced the present reality of God in a manner surpassing the normal capacity of man. God must have broken through the veil which hides Him from view and been perceived, however briefly and dimly, for what He is, for the covenant was not a theological conclusion, but rather a significant and meaningful experience, the center of the unity of Israel as the people of the Lord.[3]

The difference between an ordinary contract and the covenant becomes clearer when we realize that the prophets translate the fact of the covenant into the terms of a marriage contract. Here it is always Yahweh, the Spouse of Israel, Who takes the first step, as may be seen from Ezekiel 16:8 and Hosea 2. Therefore, the covenant does not simply come into the category of a mutual exchange of benefits. Nevertheless, there is included the idea that God will give His protection if Israel gives her obedience. With regard to the Sinai covenant, the Ten Commandments become the charter of the covenant to such an extent that the terms "covenant" and "commandments" can almost be interchanged. This testifies to the profoundly moral character of the covenant. Although Yahweh is not attached to any particular group, as Chamos was to Moab, Moloch to Ammon and Cos to Edom, between Yahweh and Israel there is a

---

[2] Paul van Imschoot, *Théologie de l'ancien testament* (Tournai: Desclée et Cie., 1954), I, 240.
[3] Theodorus C. Vriezen, *An Outline of Old Testament Theology* (London: Basil Blackwell & Mott, Ltd., 1958), p. 141.

bond which may always be violated by Israel's refusal to obey, by her sin.

In the popular religion of Israel the original idea of the covenant was often distorted so that people came to believe that Yahweh needed His people and that the fate of both parties was irrevocably linked by some sort of *natural* bond. Hence, we find the prophecies before the Exile (from the eighth to the sixth century) demanding a return to the original ethical atmosphere of the covenant. In accenting the moral demands of the covenant the prophets did not merely wish to preserve cultic traditions, but were insisting, shortly before the time of the national crisis, on the need for a profound renewal of the covenant, in the sense of an inner transformation. The old legal and cultic observances had lost their meaningful content, Israel having been unwilling to act in accordance with her promises. The last attempt to live them seriously had been in the time of Josiah in 621, and it had failed. Therefore, God decided to grant a new covenant whereby the Law would no longer be simply an external charter to be consulted, but an inner inspiration by which man would live.

Scholars speak of another covenant besides the one with Abraham and the epoch-making covenant of Sinai. This covenant to which they refer is one with Noah. They maintain that Israel's covenant obligations were primarily legal and ritual since the story of creation culminated in the institution of the Sabbath, that of the flood in the covenant with Noah and with the law concerning the sacredness of blood, and that of the covenant with Abraham in the sealing by circumcision. They also note that in some sources the ten commands are given differently and are predominantly ritual rather than moral. Also the sanctity of the Sabbath was considered as a sign of the covenant. Yet it seems clear that from the start ethical attitudes were also part of the covenant obligations of Israel.[4]

The covenant must be studied especially from the point of

[4] Bernhard W. Anderson, *Understanding the Old Testament* (Englewood Cliffs, N.J.: Prentice-Hall, Inc., 1957), p. 53.

view of its implications for Israel's theological beliefs. No aspect of Israel's faith is more conspicuous than the covenant as a basis for a continuing, redemptive relationship with God.[5] The making of the covenant at Sinai is the crucial historical event which made possible this faith whose outstanding concept is salvation. Although there were many blood covenants between clans or tribes and their respective deities in the ancient world of the Hebrews, what makes the Hebrew covenant unique is the appearance of a new conception, the idea that God was not automatically obliged upon request to help His people. The proffer of help depended upon the merits of each case, which were determined by a standard of measurement derived from the objective, righteous will of God rather than from community mores and customs, or from a sense of national identity.

The main points of the Sinai covenant as found in the Yahwistic, Elohistic, and Deuteronomic sources could then be listed as follows: the theophany to Moses on the sacred mountain; the divine promise to accompany the Hebrews across the desert and to give them a new home; the detailed requirements to govern social, economic, and religious conduct; the solemn injunction to comply or take the unpleasant consequences; and the unanimous consent of the people to the terms of the agreement.

As far as Hebrew historians and prophets are concerned, Hebrew history begins with the making of the Sinai covenant. There is the chant of gratitude and thanksgiving to the God Who will keep the covenant through all of Israel's history. Obedience or disobedience to the covenant is the criterion for judging men and events from the beginning of to the fall of Judah in 586 B.C. The new covenant was to be the constitution for the new community of a redeemed Israel. The keeper of the covenant was God, the giver of salvation.[6]

It was not Israel's righteousness that drew God to fix a cove-

[5] Walther Eichrodt, *Theology of the Old Testament*, trans. J. A. Baker (Philadelphia: Westminster Press, 1961), I, 41.
[6] Samuel J. Schultz, *The Old Testament Speaks* (New York: Harper & Row, Publishers, 1960), pp. 57-59.

nant with her. "Be assured, then, that it is not because of your goodness that the LORD your God is giving you this fine land to occupy; for you are a stiff-necked people" (Deut. 9:6). But having once chosen Israel out of the nations by a purely gratuitous act, Yahweh continues to abide by the covenant. The election of Israel is a pure mystery. It was not to be a matter of pride. God chose Israel to accomplish His purpose with her: He would educate her and use her as an instrument to establish His ultimate kingdom. The covenant He had made with Israel did not imply that He would not punish her transgressions, but that He would persist in His love for her and place at her disposal the means of loving Him.[7]

Biblical writers and editors have one decisive question to ask of history: how did Israel's leading personalities, especially its rulers, fulfill the purposes of God with respect to His covenant with the nation? The cycle of history, as the Deuteronomists saw it, contained the original revelation and covenant binding man to God Who had initiated it, followed by Israel's alternate rejection and repentance. Even man's hope for the future took concrete form in the idea of the continuing covenant community.

Many aspects of God are revealed to the Hebrew by the covenant relation. Through faithful keeping of the promises made in the covenant bond, God shows His love and kindness, and because He is a God Who keeps His covenant with His people, one can trust that God's promises are sure to be fulfilled for those who believe in Him. With the Sinai covenant, we have a theocratic kingdom, founded upon the covenant relation between God and Israel, and with this is also involved the idea that sin has highly social repercussions.

According to some authorities, there are four aspects of the main motif of Israel's religion, that is, the direct relationship

---

[7] Edmund Jacob, *Theology of the Old Testament,* trans. A. W. Heathcote and Philip J. Allcock (New York: Harper & Row, Publishers, 1958), p. 213.

between Holy God and man. These are: God's activity in history; prophecy as a revelation of the communion between the Holy One and man; the personal character of religious life; and the idea of the covenant, this last being the most influential in the Old Testament writings. As to the question of whether the doctrine of the covenant is a late theological scheme or an early historical fact, scholars today generally hold the latter view. They argue that the earliest prophetic writings (especially Hosea) agree with the two earliest historical sources (J and E) on the origin of the doctrine of the covenant, and this points to an early date for the emergence of the covenant idea.[8]

However, biblical theology is more concerned with the idea of the spiritual conception implicit in the covenant than with the date of origin of the doctrine. The relationship between Yahweh and Israel is not looked upon as natural but as initiated in history by Yahweh. This unique view proves that Israel's religion, as we find it in the Old Testament, lacks the dominant characteristic of the ancient popular religions and is, therefore, not originally a typical or popular religion. Yahweh took the initiative and this is confirmed by the fact that He is always the subject of the verb used to indicate concluding the covenant. Therefore, everything originates with and emanates from Yahweh.[9]

The implications of the doctrine of the covenant are absolute recognition of the reality of a true communion between God and man; absolute recognition of God as the Holy One, the Supreme, Who has established and guides this relationship; and acknowledgment of the rules of the covenant. The covenant is, in this way, the clearest illustration of the idea of communion with God, a fundamental element of the Old Testament message.

---

[8] G. Ernest Wright, *The Old Testament Against Its Environment* (London: S.C.M. Press, Ltd., 1957), p. 58.
[9] H. H. Rowley, *The Faith of Israel* (London: S.C.M. Press, 1956), p. 68.

With respect to the idea of kinship established by the covenant, we should also note that the theological background of the words "faithfulness," "righteousness," and "justice," without which the Israelite community could not exist, is the basic idea of the covenant. As Yahweh lives in a covenant-relation with man, man is so linked with his fellowman by *hesed* (faithfulness). Men linked together by Yahweh are brothers and must help each other. Also, like the relation between God and man, that between man and man is personal throughout. The original covenant is an election, a bond of communion, and an *obedience,* which takes concrete shape in the form of law. All subsequent covenant-makings later than Sinai are renewals or extensions to a wider association of the Sinai covenant.

Covenant also implies the idea of a mediator, for the relationships between Yahweh and the Messianic king of the future or the reigning kings are presented as a covenant. These characters, beneficiaries of the covenant, are at the same time its mediators. We need not assert that the covenant of its nature requires a mediating personality, but it is clear that, as the concept of covenant becomes more defined, the role of the mediator in the past (Moses), in the present (the king), or in the future (the Messiah), tends to be stressed. The mediatorial function can also be fulfilled by a group. In the post-Exilic period, the order of priests mediates the covenant and makes its benefits possible for the people.[10]

. The problem as to why the Sinai covenant is not mentioned so frequently in later writings can be explained by the fact that faith in Israel, while having a historical foundation, goes beyond the sheer historical events themselves, to renew itself by contact with the objective realities resulting from those events. Though a reminder of the covenant was preserved in the Feast of Tabernacles, there is a theological reason for the overshadowing of the Sinai theme by that of the Exodus. The Exodus, being

[10] Eichrodt, *Theology of the Old Testament,* p. 62.

always the classic miracle of God's action in defense of Israel, illustrated in a most expressive way that Yahweh's revelation was made through *history*.

The covenant was always a cause of consolation and strength to Israel, but it would be fruitless to deny that the idea of the covenant also carried certain dangers with it. There was the ever present temptation to regard Yahweh as forever linked to Israel by His fidelity and to forget the moral and religious obligations that the covenant imposed upon Israel. Moreover, there was in Israel a recurring danger of substituting purely ritual and cultic observances for the deeper spiritual attitudes that the covenant demanded. As Israel took over the sanctuaries of the Canaanite gods the danger increased. Popular religion tended to assume that while Yahweh, because of His covenant, guided the ultimate destinies of Israel, one might safely leave less important matters, such as harvests and rain, to the care of local deities.[11]

When the people were in need of reform, the Deuteronomists stressed election as the fundamental message and the fact that, by virtue of this election, Yahweh is the master of nature and of the nations. The prophets of the eighth century stressed the moral obligations on Israel's part which stemmed from the covenant. The reform movement of Deuteronomy channeled these obligations in closely defined laws. Israel had to be clearly marked off from the peoples whom Yahweh had not elected, and the law would be the wall of separation. Its observances would allow Israel to draw from the covenant strength and the power to witness Yahweh. After Deuteronomy, the term covenant was again used by the prophets. Now, however, a twofold orientation of the concept of covenant developed. The priests passed the limit of the primitive sense by making the covenant Israel's basic religious concept; all religious attitudes find their ulti-

---

[11] H. H. Rowley, *Rediscovery of the Old Testament* (Philadelphia: Westminster Press, 1946), p. 191.

mate justification in the covenant; all is fixed once for all, and even creation is envisaged in the light of covenant. As the chosen people were separated from the impure, so in creation there was a separation from chaos. Law, the concrete expression of the covenant, became more and more identified with it, and obedience to the covenant became obedience to the letter of the law. In the last stage of Israel's history, the term covenant came to signify the people themselves or the Jewish religion.

Later prophets, such as Jeremiah and Ezekiel, insisted very strongly upon the interiority of virtue and conformity to the demands of the covenant. Yahweh Himself will act to create a new heart in His people and to inspire them from within to observe the law in its proper spirit. He will create a new covenant which is the renewal of the old, and He will enable Israel to conform to it.[12]

Moreover, the idea of the openness of the covenant becomes more and more stressed as time goes on. Israel is to have a missionary destiny to bring the goods of the covenant to other nations. Isaiah further noted that Israel will be a source of blessing to all nations, for the suffering servant will be a light to all nations.

We might also point out that God's faithfulness receives its clearest demonstration in and through the covenant. It is because God has concluded a covenant that He has shown faithfulness. The deepening of the idea by the prophets sometimes placed the faithfulness of God beyond the covenant. This is why the breaking of the covenant by its human partners does not entail of necessity the suppression of God's faithfulness. The prophets wanted to insist upon the firm nature which always characterizes the action of God.

Finally an answer has been given to the question of why such a legal term as covenant was used in the Old Testament to refer to this direct relationship with God. It was because the Old

---

[12] Van Imschoot, *Théologie de l'ancien testament*, I, p. 245.

Testament was interested less in the nature of God than in His work, less in the existence of God than in His presence. The idea of the covenant captured God as an active power in the midst of men, a power from which they could not escape.

GOD

THE CREATOR

OF ALL

✦ ✦ ✦ ✦

CHAPTER FIVE

Before we can begin to discuss the idea of creation in the Old Testament, we must realize the relative unimportance of this speculative problem in the minds of those who wrote the inspired books. Today we are fascinated by the problem of our origins: did the world come into existence through an evolutionary process or was it created out of nothing by the *fiat* of God? In the Old Testament, on the other hand, there are really only two passages where evidence of such curiosity on the part of the Hebrews can be found: the narratives of Genesis and the poetic parallel in Psalm 104.[1] As we shall see, the faith of the Jews was, above all, practical, and the story of creation was in the service of religious truths.

Israel's starting point in the discovery of God was not nature but God Himself. In this the Israelites differed from the Greeks and the other ancient peoples of the East. Beginning with na-

---

[1] Edmund Jacob, *Theology of the Old Testament*, trans. A. W. Heathcote and Philip J. Allcock (New York: Harper & Row, Publishers, 1958), p. 138.

ture implies working back to a logically required first principle from which all plants and animals and men derive. Such a first principle, which satisfies the logical exigencies of the philosopher, was totally foreign to the Hebrews. Cosmology did not interest them. When do we first find a clearly marked concept of God the Creator? The prophets of the seventh and eighth centuries mentioned many aspects of Yahweh's power, but they relegated to second place the idea of creation.[2] It is really only in Deutero-Isaiah that the omniscience of God as Creator comes to a central position in Hebrew preaching.[3] Finally, in a relatively late portion of the Old Testament, the first creation account in Genesis, we find the full flowering of Hebrew thought on the matter.[4]

Granted that speculative and scientific considerations were not foremost in Hebrew theological thought concerning creation, what purpose did the concept of God as Creator serve?[5] Before discussing this question we should consider briefly the Hebrew concept of the universe and some Egyptian and Babylonian parallels to their beliefs on Creator and created. In this way, the uniqueness of Hebrew thought may become clearer.

The Hebrew concept of the world developed relatively late and shows many characteristics of the beliefs held by the other Oriental peoples living around Israel. The world to them was a sort of flat dish, surrounded and supported by water. Heaven was like a roof over the world and somewhere beyond that was the heaven of heavens where God lived. In the earliest times the Jewish concept of the world contained little more than the countryside familiar to a Palestinian farmer. But in the first

-

[2] Gustave Lambert, "La Création dans la Bible," *Nouvelle Revue théologique* (1953), LXXV, 252.
[3] Carrol Stuhlmueller, "The Theology of Creation in Second-Isaiah," *Catholic Biblical Quarterly* (1954), pp. 427-67.
[4] Ludwig Köhler, *Theology of the Old Testament*, A. S. Todd, trans. (Philadelphia: Westminster Press, 1957), p. 85.
[5] Frederick L. Moriarty and William G. Guindon, "Genesis and Scientific Studies on the Origin of the World," *Catholic Biblical Quarterly* (1950), pp. 429-38.

Genesis account of creation, which is later in time than the second, man has become the apex of a pyramid whose dimensions embrace the entire world. Not to be forgotten either is the role that purely artistic conceptions play in the Hebraic description of creation. Four signifies the four regions of the earth. God blesses creation three times. The phrase "God said" is repeated ten times.

Apparently Israelite ideas of creation were influenced much more by Babylonian than by Egyptian sources. And we can mark a steady purification of Israel's faith in an absolutely unique and all-powerful God from the decreasing importance given to Babylonian thought.

At the basis of all Babylonian thought lay a dualistic idea of the universe. The creation of the world was the result of a conflict between two gods who were apparently personifications of order and chaos. These two forces being more or less equal, final victory went to neither. There are indications everywhere in the Old Testament, not only of a Hebraic concept of creation similar to the Babylonian, but also of direct influences of the latter on the former. In the Ras Shamra texts from the coast of north Syria we find biblical names like Anath, who fought the dragon, El and Latan (Leviathan) and Baal. In Isaiah, for example, we read of the dragon and the serpent who had to be destroyed before the rule of God could be consummated. In the second account of creation in Genesis, God creates man as a potter builds a vase and breathes the breath of life into him; here, too, we have an ancient bit of symbolism.

The important question to be resolved concerns the uniquely Hebraic contribution and the extent to which the Old Testament writers overcame the idea of a pre-existent chaos that did battle with the Lord God and with which He had to do battle in order to protect His kingdom. On this point the authorities are in disagreement.

Some feel that the idea of creation out of nothing is foreign to the Old Testament, although they admit that the power of

God is greater in the Hebrew story than in other myths of the
time and that the only possible issue of the increasingly more
spiritual development of the Old Testament story was just such
an act of creation. But, some scholars think, at first Yahweh was
not the God of heaven and earth; to become so He had to
dethrone other deities and it took Him several centuries to
extend His power over that of the underworld. Thus Tannin
and Leviathan had to be conquered to assure God's kingdom:

> On that day will the LORD punish, with his sword which
> is hard and great and strong, Leviathan the fleeing
> serpent, Leviathan the coiled serpent; And he will
> slay the dragon that is in the sea.
> —ISAIAH 27:1

It is also thought that one can trace in the Psalms the meta-
morphosis of Leviathan from an adversary of God to a simple
plaything which the master of the universe has built for His
amusement. In the first Genesis story of creation (later in point
of view of time) God Himself creates the sea monsters, who
appear in other texts as His opponents. It is generally agreed
that because of the strict monotheism of the author of the first
Genesis account he could not have believed "tohu-wa-bohu"
(void and empty) and "tehom" (the deep) to be eternal; they too
were creatures of the one, all-powerful God.

A more conservative opinion holds that creation out of nothing is too latent, even in the earliest references to creation, to
emerge explicitly in a later, second-century text (II Macc.) in
which the mother of the seven martyred sons says:

> I beseech you, my child, to look up at the heaven and
> the earth, and see all that is in them, and perceive
> that God did not make them out of the things that existed,
> and in that way the human race came into existence.
> —II MACCABEES 7:28

In Genesis 1:2 the universe is "tohu-wa-bohu" (void and empty),
and in the verses that follow it is formed into the world as we

know it today.[6] Therefore, it is contended, the initial verse of the story, "In the beginning God created heaven and earth," is proof that God created primeval matter and "chaos." And the same viewpoint also considers the frequently reappearing antithesis between God and the world as an implication that God, standing outside the world, is its sole Creator:

> Thus says the Lord, your Redeemer, Who formed you from the womb: I, the Lord, the maker of all, Who stretched out the heavens alone, Who laid out the earth—who was with me?
>
> —ISAIAH 44:24

It is likely too that the story of Genesis 1 must be read against the background of, and as a counterstatement to, the Babylonian myth of creation from and by the gods. For the author names all the natural forces in which Babylonian sources saw the deities and then, quite bluntly, asserts that God made them.[7] Even in the most ancient Hebrew poetry which has come down to us, the idea of creation is perhaps present, at least implicitly, because God appears as master of nature (Jos. 10:13; Jth. 5:12-15; Gen. 49:25; Exod. 15:8-11; Deut. 33:14; Ps. 29). Certainly the idea of God's creative activity in bringing the world into existence is earlier in Israel's thought than is sometimes conceded. It would be surprising if Israel did not possess this concept, since so many of her neighbors regarded their gods as somehow creators. In spite of the naïve anthropomorphisms of Genesis 2, Yahweh is clearly portrayed there as the author of all that is. When later writers use the old mythological traditions of Israel's neighbors or of the popular religions of Israel, they adapt these to point up the unique transcendence of Yahweh, His limitless power and creative wisdom. In Genesis 1,

---

[6] Michael J. Gruenthaner, "The Scriptural Doctrine on First Creation," *Catholic Biblical Quarterly* (1947), IX, 48-58, 206-19, 307-20.
[7] John L. McKenzie, *The Two-Edged Sword, An Interpretation of the Old Testament* (Milwaukee: Bruce Publishing Co., 1956), pp. 77-78.

while the idea of creation *ex nihilo* is not taught formally, it is surely implicit, for Yahweh is the unique master of all the elements, and none offers resistance to the activity of God.[8]

As was mentioned at the beginning of this chapter, such purely speculative questions as creation out of nothing held little interest for the Hebrew authors of the Old Testament. Their references to creation had almost always a religious purpose, and it is this use of creation stories for a higher end that we will now attempt to illustrate.

In the Genesis stories, for example, one can discover the following doctrinal elements: The world was created by one God Who stands outside the world, and it was created by His almighty will, His spirit, and His word; The elements and stars are made by Him and are not entitled to divine veneration; Man is the crown of creation and he is to live in monogamous union with a woman; Creation exists for man's use; Man must not work on the Sabbath. Clearly, the recital of creation extols God's power and wisdom.

The key to the Babylonian myth of creation, we recall, was a struggle between deities out of which came the world. In the orderly and artistic, almost liturgical, creation story of Genesis, one sees rather the representation of the orderly labor of the workman, who pursues his craft six days of the week and rests on the seventh. Perhaps this best example of such orderly activity is not unworthy to be attributed to the Creator.

The power and freedom of God are emphasized again when He "forms" man, as a potter does the earth. In the later creation story (Gen. 1), however, God speaks, and the results are immediately produced.

But perhaps the main emphasis of the creation story is eschatological. Already, at the beginning of history, the world's end is foreshadowed, somehow promised. Creation is the necessary

---

[8] Paul van Imschoot, *Théologie de l'ancien testament* (Tournai: Desclée et Cie., 1954), I, 95.

condition for history and the covenant of God; the complete accomplishment of God's plan is in germ at the creation.

Some scholars hold that the concept of the Creator of the world was originally inseparable from that of God as Savior: God created in order to save. In Psalm 135, for example, we find united the description of God as creating and of God as acting in history:

> To him who made the heavens with skill, For his kindness
> is everlasting; To him who spread out the earth upon
> the waters, For his kindness is everlasting; To him
> who made the great lights, For his kindness is everlasting;
> The sun to rule by day, For his kindness is everlasting;
> The moon and the stars to rule by night, For his kind-
> ness is everlasting.
>
> —PSALM 135:5-9

Immediately thereafter begins the recital of God's great deeds in history:

> To him who smote the Egyptians in their first-born,
> For his kindness is everlasting; And brought forth
> Israel from the midst of them, For his kindness is
> everlasting; With a strong hand and an outstretched
> arm, For his kindness is everlasting.
>
> —PSALM 135:10-12

In Deutero-Isaiah there is clearly noted what may be called continual creation; the world is "in process" or a passage to the Kingdom of God.

The concept of creation often serves only to bolster the faith of the Jewish people so they may trust in God's mercy or in His power to intervene in history. In Isaiah, for example, we read:

> Why should you say, O Jacob, And speak, O Israel:
> My way is hidden from the LORD, And my rights are
> passed over by my God? Have you not known? Have you
> not heard? The LORD is a God everlasting, The Creator
> of the ends of the earth. He does not faint, nor grow
> weary; His insight is unfathomable. He gives power

to the fainting, and to him that has no might he
increases strength.
                                        —ISAIAH 40:27-29

The covenant of God with Israel is the goal of creation and serves as its internal basis. God created the world for the covenant, for by means of Israel, love and salvation were to come to humanity; therefore, creation is both the condition and the consequence of the covenant. Faith in God the Savior is more important than faith in God the Creator and is more often and more directly the object of the faith of the Israelites.

The concept of God acting in history provides us with the deepest explanation of why Yahweh the Creator could never have been for the Hebrews a simple first cause: He was too involved in bringing to a good end the work He had begun with creation. The Jewish people had not found God—He Himself had searched them out to be His people.

There seems to be relatively more agreement than disagreement among authorities as to what the Old Testament Jews meant by creation and as to the sources and developments of their belief. What emerges most clearly is that the idea of creation in itself, abstractly considered, did not become important to the Jews until fairly late—perhaps in the second century before Christ. Creation for the Jews was a religious concept or, more properly, was in the service of religious ideas and preaching. Indicating the power of God and His consequent ability to intervene in order to help the Jews against their enemies; this concept of creation shows us the wisdom and mercy of God, and therefore His willingness to forgive a repentant people.

Most important of all, creation was historical and, ultimately, eschatological: creation came about *for the sake of the covenant.* And it is to the covenant that the Jews advert continually. God has chosen the Jewish people, and for this choice the existence of the earth and peoples upon it was a precondition; therefore, God created. But what was of practical importance was God's choice and the commands He laid upon His people, their obedience and disobedience. Creation was at best a subordinate idea.[9]

[9] John L. McKenzie, "God and Nature in the Old Testament," *Catholic Biblical Quarterly* (1952), pp. 18-39, 124-45. Cf. also John L. McKenzie, "The Hebrew Attitude Towards Mythological Polytheism," *Catholic Biblical Quarterly* (1952), pp. 323-35.

THE LOVE OF
GOD

✛ ✛ ✛ ✛

C H A P T E R S I X

One might almost say that the whole story of Israel is simply the development of the theme "With an everlasting love have I loved you" (Jer. 31:3). The entire history of the Jewish people is the history of God's love for His chosen ones, with the climax reached outside the Old Testament, in the Messiah, for the love of God in the Old Testament remains an unfinished concept.[1] Yet, at the outset we must make a distinction: While it is true that God's love in the Old Testament is central to the spiritual relation of Israel to her Lord, this love, as an attribute, is not clearly separable from the many other attributes of God.

It is a normal feature of "primitive" languages that there are many expressions, with various shades of meaning, to indicate a concept that, in a language like English, is denoted by a single word. In ancient Greek, for example, there is an astounding variety of words for the verb "to know," each indicating a special feature of the idea of knowing. In the course of time,

---

[1] John L. McKenzie, *The Two-Edged Sword, An Interpretation of the Old Testament* (Milwaukee: Bruce Publishing Co., 1956), p. 293.

through a universalizing process, some of the Homeric and pre-Homeric verbs for "to know" fell into disuse, and certain other verbs accreted to themselves the meanings that had formerly been expressed by them. Much the same was true of ancient Hebrew, as far as the "fragmentation" of meanings is concerned. No *one* word in the Bible was employed to express "love," since the varying peripheral associations of a particular concept demanded various special words.

The two words *hesed* and *'ahab* are worthy of discussion because of their frequent use and also because they describe the two main types of divine love that have been given emphasis in the Old Testament.

The noun *hesed* is usually translated by the expressions "steadfast love" or "loving kindness"; but, as we have seen, there is no adequate English word or phrase to express the full meaning of the concept. There are a number of elements in *hesed:* faithfulness, mercy, pity, goodness, and piety. Primarily, the love described by *hesed* is "covenant-love," the love of God for Israel that implies His unanswering loyalty to her. There are, however, other notions that extend this concept of *hesed.* Some authorities emphasize the kindness and favor of God, his "spirit of helpfulness." Others underscore the "outreaching" character and link the word with God's redemptive power. Still others suggest that the "kindness" aspect of the concept is characteristic of God's piety, and connect it with the word "faithfulness." Finally, almost all scholars admit that *hesed*-love involves a note of condescension, since it is the love of a superior for an inferior.

If *hesed* is the word that describes the steadfast love of God in keeping faith with the covenant, *'ahab* might be called the love of God which impelled Him to make the covenant in the first place. If we call *hesed* "covenant-love," we might use the phrase "election-love" to specify *'ahab,* for it was an unconditioned, completely free act of God to choose the Jewish nation as His people. This election of the Jews as a chosen people reflects an essential mystery of love, for we cannot explain God's choice by the fact that the Jews were worthier than any other race.

As far as a definition of the word itself is concerned, we may say that *'ahab* is a noun used for "pure and simple love." Although *'ahab* like *hesed* generally indicates the love of a superior for an inferior, it can also be used to describe a love between equals. There is a strong notion of vehement desire involved; and, therefore, in its own peculiar way, it partakes of both *eros* and *agape*. Snaith claims that *'ahab* was used for any and every kind of love, being unconditional and limited only by the nature of the lover.[2] There is, however, an exception. *'Ahab* was never used to refer to the love of wife and husband or child and parent. To the Hebrew mind, the marriage relationship of husband and wife and the relationship between parent and offspring included too much of the ideas of authority and duty to be encompassed by *'ahab*.

The Old Testament also speaks of Yahweh's "compassionate love" for Israel. The Hebrew word employed here is closely related to the word for "womb" and suggests the love of a mother for her child. Applied to the idea of divine love, this word is a particularly forceful one and used by Jeremiah with great effect (Jer. 16:5). This compassion, when it is divine, is the mercy of God that directs Him to hear the pleas of men and have pity on them. In a sense, it is the "mother-love" of God. We might particularize its meaning even more by saying that compassionate love is the mercy and love of God directed toward the poor and needy, as well as the repentant sinner. There is a continual history of this compassion and mercy of God throughout the Old Testament, striking examples of which occur in the Psalms, especially 77:9; 79:8; 86:5; 119:77.

There are also several other words related to the idea or concept of love, and while none of these could actually be translated by the word love they are so close in meaning that they deserve at least passing reference. The word to join or to attach oneself to something is often employed to indicate the reality of the bond between God and Israel (cf. Deut. 7:7; Ps. 91:14). The "long-suffering" love of God refers to His mercy in delaying a sinner's punishment. The expression "to take pleasure in" is more properly used of human love in the Old Testament and does not especially characterize Yahweh's love. Finally, *yada'*, the Hebrew word for a special sense of "know," is used to indicate the way in which a husband knew his wife in love (e.g., Adam knew Eve).

While it is true then that there is no one word in the Bible which would serve adequately to describe the love of God, there are, however, two words which deserve more detailed treatment: *hesed* and *'ahab*. Since we have already treated of *hesed* elsewhere, we shall discuss it here only as it is found representing covenant-love in the writings of some of the prophets. *'Ahab* also only begins to receive a full treatment in Prophetic literature; therefore, we shall limit our treatment of this word to the late period.

For the brief historical discussion we intend to make, it would seem wise to restrict our investigation of the "early" development of the notion of the love of God to a general summary. The process of development might be summarized briefly as follows: In the earlier books of the Old Testament God's love is seen almost exclusively from the viewpoint of His favors to Israel. He manifests His love by the great deeds He does to deliver Israel from calamity and to ensure her prosperity. In the later documents Israel's religious perspective is broadened and God's love is more universal. More frequent references are found to His love for all mankind and even for the world of creaturedom as a whole.[3] Not only does there seem to have been a change from a parochialism to a more universal application of the love of God, but also, with time, the nature of the

---

[3] Charles Piepenbring, *Theology of the Old Testament* (New York: Thomas Y. Crowell Company, 1893), p. 119.

deep spiritual relationship between God and Israel became
more and more vivid and meaningful. There is a very definite
move toward a more personal idea of God's love, especially with
such prophets as Hosea and Isaiah. The idea of the loving God
which we draw from Deuteronomy bears real fruit in the writings of the later period:

> It was not because you were the greatest of all peoples
> that the LORD set his heart on you and chose you
> (for you were the smallest of all peoples), but it was
> because the LORD loves you, and would keep the oath
> that he swore to your fathers, that the LORD brought
> you out by a strong hand, and rescued you from a
> state of slavery, from the power of Pharaoh, king of
> Egypt. . . . He will love you, bless you, and multiply
> you; he will bless the offspring of your body and the
> produce of your soil, your grain and the wine and
> oil, the issue of your cattle, and the progeny of your
> flock, in the land which he swore to your fathers to
> give you.
>   —DEUTERONOMY 7:7-8, 13

With the coming of the eighth-century prophets and their
successors, the Old Testament is more concerned with the *moral*
relationship between Yahweh and Israel. At this point, it would
be well to gain an understanding of the historical setting of the
period. The writing prophets began their work about 750 B.C.,
at a time when Israel was in grave peril. The northern kingdom
was to fall in 721 B.C.; but at midcentury there was sufficient
prosperity for the people to be distracted from the dangers from
within and without. The Jewish people were turning away
from God, and Assyria threatened the very existence of Israel
as a nation. Hosea felt most deeply this idolatry and infidelity of
the chosen people to their God and preached the message of
God's love as an antidote to it. After the fall of Samaria, Isaiah
and Micah in the kingdom of Judah gave that southern part of
Israel a brief period of safety. Eventually, however, Jerusalem
was besieged (701 B.C.). Although the siege was lifted in 700 B.C.,
the danger remained. In the seventh century things went from

bad to worse, and the question of whether or not God would
abandon His people seemed a real one. The prophet Jeremiah,
seeing destruction closing in, urged reform in religion, but instead witnessed the collapse of the state and died a lonely death.
In 586 B.C. Jerusalem finally fell to the Babylonians and the
Jewish people went into exile. In this period two prophets,
Ezekiel and "Deutero-Isaiah," rose to comfort Israel and renew a spirit of hopefulness for the future. By the end of the
sixth century, Israel was ready to make a fresh start.

During this era in the history of the chosen people, the
theology of love received its most striking development. The
last great step was taken before the New Testament presentation of the message of love by Christ. Hosea, perhaps more than
anyone else—even though he is a "minor" prophet—prepared
the way for the teaching of Jesus on this subject with his
poignant portrayal of the love of God. Isaiah was deeply aware
of man's unworthiness because of sin; and, by his comparison
of man's humble state with the supreme holiness of God, the
love of God took on another degree of importance. Deutero-
Isaiah emphasized the spiritual relationship of God to Israel and
to the nations, and it was not until the teaching of this prophet
that Yahweh's gracious purpose to the world as a whole was
made a cardinal theme of prophetic teaching. The full blossom-
ing of the theme of the love of God for all mankind, including
even the heathen, in persuasive and affective expression is
found only in Jonah; but it was through the teaching of
Deutero-Isaiah that, in a sense, the first real movement toward
this was begun. In Jeremiah we have a testimony to a final
aspect of the love of God: its relation to the individual man
rather than to the group hitherto unmentioned by the other
prophets.

In the treatments of the notion of God's love prior to Hosea's
examination of it, there was always a strong element of the idea
of law and covenant, insofar as the love of God for Israel was a
contract. Such an approach, however, had its inadequacies, and
it took the new discussion of the love of Yahweh by Hosea to

give the whole conception a more inward and personal direction. His revitalization of the subject of divine love was, in its way, revolutionary. The message had always been there in germ, but he was the one to dramatize and clarify it. Hosea employed both words, *hesed* and *'ahab*, the former to designate the most sublime type of divine love, and the latter to refer to the "lower" manifestations of Yahweh's love. This prophet developed the theme of the *gratuitous* nature of God's love.[4]

Hosea is frequently compared by scholars to Amos. As Amos developed the idea of divine justice and gave it new significance, so Hosea spurred the development of Israel's consciousness of divine love. His teaching marks a definite stage of growth, but it should not be misconstrued as having no roots in Israel's past history. What had, after all, given rise to the religion of Israel was an election of love on God's part, and the mighty event of the Exodus fixed forever in Israel's memory the love and tenderness of God. All her victories in battle were due to God's love for Israel, and she was well aware that it was through this loving care of God that she had conquered the Canaanites and the Philistines. The covenant itself was a supreme sign of God's devotion to Israel and was not merely the expression of a legal relationship between Israel and God, but of a relationship of love. The fundamental idea that lay behind it was not juridical obligation but God's gracious good will. Hosea's contribution was to stress the notes of tenderness, gratuity, and fidelity that mark God's love for Israel.

The story of Hosea's personal life is intimately connected with his teaching on love, and it serves as its most important illustration. Several times in the Old Testament God seems to work through His prophets and holy men in a special way, forging their lives, as it were, into living symbols of a deep spiritual reality.[5] In Hosea's case, God's desire seemed to have been to

---

[4] Jacques Guillet, *Themes of the Bible* (South Bend: Fides Publishers, 1960), pp. 51-54.
[5] Frederick L. Moriarty, *Introducing the Old Testament* (Milwaukee: Bruce Publishing Co., 1960), p. 115.

draw from the prophet's marriage a universal message about the nature of the marriage between Himself and His people. As the story is told, prescinding from its historicity or not, Hosea was married to a woman who became unfaithful to him and degraded herself to the position of a prostitute. When Hosea learned of his situation, God instructed him to forgive his wife and to receive her back into his love. After this was done, he deeply realized the remarkable parallel between his personal experience and the relationship between Yahweh and Israel. Just as his wife had been unfaithful to him, so Israel had been unfaithful to her divine spouse by practicing idolatry; and just as he was able to forgive his wife and accept her back into his love, so God's love for Israel was so great that He could receive her back and forgive her infidelity.

The experience of Hosea is significant for several reasons. First of all, by strong implication, idolatry is equated in his writings with harlotry. Second, the figure of God as the spouse of Israel is stressed, and the nature of His love is further explained by placing it in this context. In the framework of Jewish custom and practice, the husband was, it is true, an authoritarian figure, and the duty of the wife to her spouse was uppermost. There is, however, a strong note of intimacy involved when we speak of the marriage of Yahweh and the Jewish people; the warm affection of God is certainly stressed, although the role of authoritarian is not absent. Yahweh had in the past been married to His people by virtue of the covenant, and Israel, like Hosea's wife, had been unfaithful to the "marriage vows." By welcoming the Jewish nation back into His favor, Yahweh was making a gesture that she did not deserve. Finally, as the Jewish husband was responsible for the education of his wife, so God was involved in the teaching of the Jewish people. It was through the prophets in particular that this idea of education developed in the framework of a general eschatological orientation.

When Hosea employed the figure of Yahweh as the husband of Israel, he was taking up a theme that was not new in ancient

Eastern literature, but he gave the theme a new significance. Israel was already familiar with the theme from her pagan neighbors, for it was current among them to conceive of the local god as wedded to his land and his people. But Hosea purged the idea of the grosser associations it had in other religions and gave it a highly ethical significance.

Hosea was not only concerned with expressing the nature of divine love through the metaphor of the marriage relation, for he also employed the figure of the father-son union to explain further the mystery of Yahweh's love. Just as Israel could be considered as the wife of Yahweh, so it could also be looked upon as His son. The main point of this metaphor, scholars seem to agree, was that God was "Father" in the sense of being the Creator, Lord, and Guardian of His people. We should not, of course, think of the notion of fathership in all its Christian implications, for this is not the way in which the Old Testament usage of this figure is meant to be taken. Hosea is by no means the only Scriptural writer to employ this expression to describe the relationship existing between Yahweh and His people. There are numerous instances of almost similar uses of the term (e.g. Jer. 3:4, 19; Isa. 63:16; Deut. 32:6; Ps. 68:5, 89; 27; Mal. 1:6; 2:10 ff.), and in most cases there is almost as strong a notion of affection involved as in the figure of the marriage. The notion of divine fathership means especially that particular spiritual relationship between Yahweh and Israel through which, by a series of gracious acts, He shaped and cared for it as a nation. Again, as in the metaphor of the marriage, there is a powerful element of authority and duty implicit in the idea. Despite this element of authority, the idea of tenderness generally prevails in the Old Testament usage of this metaphor. In the ten or eleven instances where Yahweh is referred to as a father or Israel as a son, pity and mercy are underscored. While the paternity of God was directed primarily to the nation and, not until very late, to the individual, still we cannot doubt that the individual Hebrew felt himself very much guided by Yahweh's paternal providence, even from the earliest times.

This idea of the fatherhood of God was not, of course, restricted to Israel. Pagan peoples, however, usually conceived their gods as fathers of the clan or people in a physical sense. Such a concept is utterly foreign to Israel, to whom communion with God was conceivable only on the basis of His gracious desire to enter into communion and never on the basis of physical descent. To Israel, the fatherhood of God was simply another expression of His gracious love for His people.

If we wish to assess the importance of Hosea in the development of the notion of divine love, we would have to conclude that, although this prophet's message was revolutionary in a sense, the essential difference between him and his predecessors was one of degree rather than of kind. The main ideas amplified by him were actually present in previous Old Testament literature, but they needed the dramatic presentation that they received at his hands.

Some of the later prophets after Hosea are just as significant for the general progress of our discussion. Jeremiah made the important connection between the love of God for the individual and the old type of religion based on nationalism. In the historical situation in which he lived, Jeremiah translated the message of the love of God for Israel into one of deliverance and guidance at a time of crisis.

Isaiah, like Jeremiah, presented his message in its special relation to historical circumstances. This prophet added another figure to the expression of the notion of the loving God: he compared God's love for Israel to the love of a mother embracing a child who has strayed from her. In fact, Yahweh's love is greater than mother-love, for the prophet asks:

> Can a woman forget her sucking child, so as not
> to have pity upon the son of her womb? Even should
> these forget, yet I will not forget you.
>
> —ISAIAH 49:15

Actually the word used by Isaiah for love in this case is more properly translated by pity or mercy, for it is derived from *rahamim* and indicates the special relation that exists between a mother and her child. The implication in Isaiah's statement seems to be that the love of God for Israel is even stronger and more steadfast than the love of a mother for her own child. Although Isaiah employed other words to indicate the love relationship (e.g. grace and favor), these are much less affectionate in their connotation and describe rather the love of a superior for an inferior.

In Deutero-Isaiah a new aspect of the love of God is presented. In a very real sense, many of the old figures and expressions are summarized in his writing, for he spoke of God as father (Isa. 43:6), creator (43:1, 15; 44:2, 24; 45:11; 51:13; 54:5), husband (50:1; 54:56), mother (49:15), and, in general, as the guardian and protector of the Jewish nation. Deutero-Isaiah was aware, just as the earlier prophets and holy men had been, of the constant loving care of Yahweh for Israel, but he broadened this idea, extending it to the whole world. Whereas Hosea, for all his masterful presentation of God's love for Israel, had little to say of the love of God for other nations, Deutero-Isaiah represented God as extending His providential concern over *all* nations. The peoples of all the world will come to Jerusalem for light and guidance. The Servant of the Lord will be a light to the Gentiles. God's love embraces all creation.

It was Jonah's contribution to express in most appealing and human fashion the love of Yahweh for the heathen. Sulking and angry at God's merciful gesture in sparing Nineveh, the prophet represented the narrow particularism of Israel. But Yahweh's concern and pity is greater than man's imaginings. He almost apologized for His own tenderheartedness as He justified to Jonah His merciful love of even the heathens.[6]

A separate chapter could be devoted to a treatment of the Psalms and even the early books of the Bible. But it has seemed best to concentrate upon Hosea and the other prophets, for through them we are able to perceive the way in which a

[6] Albert C. Knudson, *The Religious Teaching of the Old Testament* (Nashville: Abingdon Press, 1918), p. 187.

doctrine of the love of God receives its fullest Old Testament development. To be sure, the Old Testament ideas see their day of full glory only in the teaching of Christ; but, in their own way, men like Hosea and Isaiah anticipated Our Lord's teaching on the love of God.

From Genesis onward, the Old Testament presents God in a number of different ways. He is a just God, a holy God, a loving God, and, at times, an angry God. In the process of attempting to uncover the meaning of the phrase "loving God," certain side-lights were cast on other themes of Scripture, such as the Providence of God and the covenant between Yahweh and His people. In a very real sense, an investigation of any one of the attributes of God in the Old Testament leads to almost all His other attributes, as well as to some of the major ideas of Scripture. This is necessarily so because of the fact that no side or attribute of God is separable from the whole.

THE WRATH OF

GOD

✝ ✝ ✝ ✝

CHAPTER SEVEN

The Old Testament's idea of God is that of a living, present,
and active power. It never doubts the reality of God's wrath.
His anger may be directed against the heathen or against Israel
herself, but it is always a reality to be reckoned with. When men
disobey the moral will of Yahweh, His wrath is the answer to
their action. It is the worst stupidity to believe that Yahweh
cannot be angered. Because His sovereignty is absolute it cannot be flaunted with impunity. When it is flaunted, His wrath
"rises up" or is "found out" or "sent forth." It is interesting to
note that even the prophets who spoke most tenderly of God's
love, such as Hosea and Jeremiah, had no doubts about the reality
of His wrath. The day of salvation for the faithful Israelite will
also be a day of wrath for the sinner who has offended the
covenant love of God.

There are some scholars who neglect to consider this topic of
wrath formally and who present it attached to another subject,
for example, "The Holiness of God in the Old Testament,"

"The Jealousy of God in the Old Testament," or "The Righteousness of God in the Old Testament." Others devote much
time to the apparent antinomies in the concept.

In general this chapter will consist of a three-part analysis
discussing the biblical nature and expression of the wrath of
God, some traditional accusations leveled against the "demonic"
and "capricious" wrath of God, and some traditional answers
defending the just and holy wrath of God.

There are many places in the Old Testament in which the
wrath of God is made manifest. Despite this abundance, however, the expressions used to reveal this anger are, for the most
part, stereotyped, physiological phrases. The most frequently
employed terms appear to be: breath, heat, to be warm, out-
burst, overflowing passion or violence.

Some authorities hold that these words are no mere meta-
phoric elevation of man's passion and anger to the level of the
divine but a revelation of God's anger as a uniquely divine
wrath, which is derived neither from man nor from foreign
deities, that is, which owes its origins neither to anthropomor-
phism nor to syncretism. Occasional scholars, however, present
an almost antithetical view holding that the divine wrath is
akin to human passion, and is not always thought of as con-
trolled by justice, but as able to overleap the bonds of equity.
This view, however, is irreconcilable with Israel's concept of
the holiness and justice of Yahweh. Most of the texts which
speak of God's wrath make it quite clear that His anger is in
response to man's insulting behavior (e.g., Exod. 9:14; Num.
11:33; Ps. 91:10; 106:29).

Yahweh's anger is not the unmotivated anger that can be discerned in the stories of Israel's neighbors. The anger of the gods
at the flood in the Gilgamesh epic has no parallel in Old Testament history. The general tendency of the Old Testament is
rather to connect the anger of God with moral or religious
motivation. It is the rebellion of man against His holy will that
calls out the divine wrath. Suffering and death are related to sin

in the Old Testament and are not merely some capricious punishment meted out to men by the gods.[1]

It is well to notice that while the expressions employed biblically to express an exclusively divine wrath do betray strong anthropomorphic elements and may stem from Canaanite sources, Yahweh's wrath is never presented as unreasonable. Then, too, divine wrath does not necessitate a wrath which would be appropriate for the Platonic Ideal or the Aristotelian Unmoved Mover. The Hebraic God of the Old Testament is neither an idea nor one Who is unmoved. He is one Who "intervenes to punish or reward." To fulfill this mission of worldly retribution, He employs at random the serpent, the seraphim, fire and the wind, the devil, the plague, drought and war.

Traditional and scholarly accusations against a demonic and capricious wrath of God point to several Old Testament stories as evidence. Since it is neither possible nor profitable to present a detailed analysis of each view, we shall attempt a brief synopsis of the most important and most striking opinions. However awkward this approach, it seems the most logical and most orderly method possible.

There is, first of all, the view that wrath is a normal part of the irrationality and mysteriousness in God, for there are occasions when it takes very little to provoke His anger (II Sam. 24:2). "The anger of the Lord was again kindled against Israel and stirred up David among them, saying: 'Go, number Israel and Judah.' " No reason is given in the text for the anger of God. The census is seen, however, as a lack of confidence in God, Who was responsible for the growth and prosperity of Israel and Who had promised to her a progeny as numerous as the sands of the sea. In stating that it was God Who incited David to take the census, the text is probably simply ascribing to

---

[1] George A. F. Knight, *A Christian Theology of the Old Testament* (London: S.C.M. Press, Ltd., 1959), p. 131.

Yahweh the choice of David, as the Old Testament often does
ascribe to Him the free decisions of men. Since the calamities
that befall mankind are universally due to God's anger, it must
have been God Who provoked David to this fault so that He
might punish Israel or try her fidelity. In the story of Exodus
4:24-26, it seems probable that God's anger broke forth, not
without reason, but to impress upon Israel the importance of
the rite of circumcision.[2]

Another view looks on Israel's God as the supreme obstacle to
the nation's self-chosen path. It is believed by some that He
attacks His people's hopes and purposes, lashes out at their
leaders, and excoriates and condemns the Jews in unequivocal
language for their own salvation.

A third view inclines to the opinion that Yahweh's jealousy
and wrath are a "defense mechanism" and, as such, an important feature of the concept of God, an efficient safeguard
against the perils of syncretism, toward which Israel had a fatal
proclivity.

A fourth view characterizes the God of Israel as showing unjust favoritism to the cause of the Patriarchs (Gen. 12:10-20)
and as acting capriciously (I Kings 6:19-20). Those who looked
upon the Ark, the concrete symbol of Yahweh, without due
reverence are slain, but Yahweh's wrath is not unmotivated.
It is a punishment for lack of reverence, for a ritual offense.

Finally, there is the opinion that the modern western world
cannot appreciate the holiness of God and cultic sins (I Sam.
6:20) and, therefore, deserves to experience the wrath of God.

In spite of such diversity of view, it seems necessary to indicate the fact that for the most part all these accusations center
upon certain key passages. Again and again scholars cite and
discuss the same biblical verses. Invariably these are Exodus
4:24, I Kings 6:19, and II Kings 24:1.

Obviously passages such as the above should be neither ig-

---

[2] Paul van Imschoot, *Théologie de l'ancien testament* (Tournai: Desclée et Cie.,
1954), I, 88.

nored nor abused, for in their glimpses of Old Testament life
and religion, they reveal aspects of the God of Israel that stress
His closeness to Israel and His intensely personal character.
This is the living God of Israel and while He is the God of
Isaiah, Jeremiah, and Hosea, He is, in a certain sense, also the
God of Exodus, Judges, and Kings. The Hebrew will affirm the
absolute identity and singularity of Yahweh, let Jeremiah's understanding of God's wrath will obviously be more developed
than the concept of His wrath in Exodus.

The positive attributes of the wrath of God in the Old Testament provide the most extensive area of analysis. These are the
attributes that evince an historical evolution and the growth of
religious awareness.

The most primitive of the positive attributes of the wrath
of God may be said to be the immutability and permanence of
the divine hatred, the attribute that Luther emphasized as man's
burden by reason of his sin and corruption. Since God is eternal
righteousness, He hates sin by His very nature, and, hence,
there is everlasting enmity between sin and God.

In discussing God's wrath, one must take into account the
jealousy and the holiness of God. Concomitant with this holiness
is the belief in the religious exclusiveness of Israel. God is holy
and so Israel must be too, for the Holy One of Israel must be
"betrothed not to a harlot but to a virgin." By viewing the relationship of God to Israel as one of love and holiness, one sees
the wrath of God as the righteous jealousy and indignation of
the insulted bridegroom:

> Therefore, O harlot, hear the word of the Lord.
> . . . .
> I will judge you, as women are judged who break
> wedlock and shed blood, and I will turn you over to
> my bloody fury and indignation.
> —EZEKIEL 16:35, 38

Again, in considering God's anger, one may be inclined to
stress the sovereignty of God. Concomitant with sovereignty
is the notion of the service of Israel to God since He is the

Lord and Israel the servant. By viewing the relation of God to
Israel as one of master and servant, one sees the wrath of God
as an instrument of punishment toward the unruly underling.

> Take care lest you be deceived into turning aside to
> serve alien gods and to pay homage to them, and the
> anger of the LORD blaze against you, and he shut up
> the skies so that there be no rain, and the land
> yield no produce, and you quickly perish off the fine
> land that the LORD is about to give you.
> —DEUTERONOMY 11:16-17

The wrath of God as viewed thus far is immutable, resulting
from holiness, righteousness, and sovereignty. However, the
wrath of God is not entirely implacable.[3] There are several
clear instances in which God's anger is placated, not the least
of which are found in Isaiah:

> Comfort, O comfort my people, says your God; Speak
> to the heart of Jerusalem, and call to her, that
> her time of service is ended, that her guilt is paid
> in full, that she has received of the LORD's hand
> double for all her sins.
> —ISAIAH 40:1-2

and in Jeremiah:

> If a man divorce his wife, and she leave him, and
> become the wife of another man, can she return to
> him again? Is not that woman wholly polluted?
> But you have played the harlot with many lovers,
> and would fain return to me! is the oracle of the
> LORD.
> —JEREMIAH 3:1

In addition to the mutability of God's wrath, there seems to
be an historical development in the method and technique of
placating God. Scholars have noticed that in the early books of
the Old Testament, God's wrath is allayed by atonement; in

---

[3] Hermann Schultz, *Old Testament Theology* (Edinburgh: T. & T. Clark, 1898),
II, 176.

the intermediate books, it is through the prophets that God
pardons and saves; and in the final books, especially Isaiah and
Jeremiah, God pardons out of mercy and love:

> I, I, am he who for my own sake blots out your trans-
> gressions, and will remember your sins no more.
> —ISAIAH 43:25

Along with this development of God's mercy, there is also a
gradual revelation of the importance of the individual. As one
reads further into the Bible, one no longer finds the bystander
condemned for purely ritual or cultic offenses, or the offspring
condemned for community or paternal misdeeds; rather it is the
individual who stands before God.

> Therefore, O house of Israel, I will judge you each in
> accordance with his ways, is the oracle of the LORD
> God. Repent, then, and turn from all your trans-
> gressions, lest your iniquity bring you to ruin.
> —EZEKIEL 18:30

This is an enormous development in the significance of the
human personality, and the growth in individual awareness and
worth is matched by a growth in the mercy and love of the Lord.
It almost seems as if the former demands the latter; otherwise,
the reality of the person would forever be submerged beneath
cultic and tribal restrictions, beneath religious and social op-
pression, and beneath the wrath and fear of the Lord.

The historical evolution of God's wrath and God's mercy
and the historical evolution of the significance of the human
person reach a pinnacle in the "suffering servant of Yahweh"
who "is not himself guilty," yet "bears this suffering in faith,
love, and hope, . . . enduring the wrath of God for the sake
of others."

Little else can be said of wrath or mercy. Like Job, the suffering servant is guiltless; but unlike Job, his suffering is "redemptive" in that others "harvest" what he has sown. The idea
that suffering is purposeful crowns any analysis of the wrath of
God in the Old Testament, since with this notion one need not

speak merely of justice or mercy, love, and righteousness, but one can also include "the unrevealed plan of God."

When Israel violated the covenant, she incurred God's wrath, but His wrath lasts only for a time and is wholly directed to the salvation of Israel. His wrath is temporary; His fidelity is lasting. "For though there be a moment in his wrath, there is a lifetime in his favor" (Ps. 30:5). His anger reveals His righteousness; the judgments He brings upon men do not detract from His love.

Nowhere is the anger of God more evident than in the story of the flood. The anger of God is such that the whole creation deserves to be blotted out, and yet, even here, His desire to save predominates. One must follow the whole history of the Old and the New Testament before he can grasp the ultimate resolution of the tension between God's wrath and His love.

GOD

IS FAITHFUL

✠ ✠ ✠ ✠

CHAPTER EIGHT

At the center of the relationships between the God of the Old Testament and the people of Israel lies the notion of God's fidelity, His steadfast-love, His *hesed*. In immediately assigning an English equivalent to this word, we are perhaps advancing too quickly, for the notion of *hesed* is one of the richest in meaning of all the ideas of the Old Testament (see Chap. 7 for a discussion of *hesed* meaning the steadfast love of God). The demands of language force us to find some equivalent, however, for what is, in fact, an extremely complicated set of relationships: faithfulness, mercy, justice, love, the covenant, forgiveness. It is only when we have seen the connection between such ideas and the word *hesed* that we can use an equivalent expression with real significance.

As is usual, some disagreement exists among authorities concerning the derivation of the word. There has been a double development, that is, as the word relates to God and as it refers to man.[1] The Arabic term, to which this word may be traced,

---

[1] Norman H. Snaith, *The Distinctive Ideas of the Old Testament* (London: The Epworth Press, 1944, p. 94). Cf. also Remberg Sorg, *Hesed and Hasid in the Psalms* (St. Louis: Pio Decimo Press, 1953).

is usually given as *hashada* which means "to assemble with reference to a guest." Both in Arabic and in Hebrew the root has multiple meanings, not only including "to assemble" and "to envy," but also "to be hard." [2] In Hebrew the primitive meaning of the root is "strength." But it also has a special reference to the covenant, and in this way the primitive meanings of eagerness, stability, and steadfastness are brought out. It is also interesting to note that "man of *hesed*" is often the Hebrew expression for a saint or holy person. It is further important to realize that the word grows in meaning. To investigate all the eventual developments of this word is the work of the remainder of this chapter. A few preliminary words on its translation from the Hebrew will perhaps be enlightening.

It should be noted that despite the numerous studies of the word *hesed,* it still remains difficult to render it into any of our western languages. The first recorded translation into a western tongue occurs in the Septuagint.[3] The seventy emissaries did not adopt a narrow approach in translating it. The word most often used in Greek for it is *eleos,* which might itself be translated as mercy or pity. However, the nuances of meaning revealed by context are extremely varied and indicate a fundamental difference in the understanding of the term. The Vulgate follows the idea of *eleos* by translating it as *misericordia.* In English, both the Authorized Version of the Bible and the Revised Version use the term "loving kindness." The Revised Standard Version, however, prefers "steadfast love," thereby including the basic notions of strength and faithfulness. Modern scholarship, while noting its delicate shades of meaning, would offer "sure-love" or "covenant-love" as the best translation. This, it must be noted, is a rendering of *hesed* as it refers to God Himself. When it is used of man, it often sums up the filial, docile piety of the believer toward his God. Thus, it includes both

---

[2] Edmund Jacob, *Theology of the Old Testament,* trans. A. W. Heathcote and Philip J. Allcock (New York: Harper & Row, Publishers, 1958), p. 103.

[3] Ceslaus Spicq, *Agape: Prolegomènes à une étude de théologie néo-testamentaire* (Louvain, Bel.: Nauwelaerts, 1955), p. 121.

love and duty to the will of God, a combination of the qualities of Virgil's *Aeneas*, and a respect for God. The man of fidelity, of *hesed*, is he who seeks to do his pious, humble duty toward God. This is the man who maintains fidelity, but it is only because of his steadfast loyalty that he has possessed this virtue. Even at that we are told that ". . . all man's [*hesed*] is like a morning cloud, or like the dew that leaves early" (Hos. 6:4). In this statement we see suggested an important nuance of *hesed* in the Old Testament, namely, that in its fullness and permanence, it belongs only to God. It is, in fact, more than something that merely *belongs* to God; it is one of the essential aspects of God Himself.

The idea of justice and holiness being perfected in God occurs continually throughout the Old Testament and is, consequently, familiar to the Christian. But the notion of fidelity is also connected with these concepts. Hosea, comparing God's relationship with Israel to that of a man to his bride, said that God will betroth Himself to Israel ". . . in righteousness and justice . . ." (Hos. 2:19). Some scholars put special emphasis on this connection and state that the full revelation of God's justice is had in the fulfillment of His promises, in His fidelity.[4] Divine fidelity is then identified with *hesed*. Others connect this divine faithfulness or *hesed* with the divine holiness. Either way the attribute of faithfulness is attached to the idea of the Holy One of Israel in virtue of its ethical meaning. Thus *hesed* depends upon the ethical character of the divine holiness. But what of itself—in what does it consist?

In examining the root meanings of *hesed* we saw that one of its earlier meanings in Hebrew was that of strength. This is the strength which binds together two people or God and man. It is important to underscore this idea of strength; it should not be buried under the weight of the other aspects of the word's meaning. Although its essential qualities of forgiveness and

---

[4] Paul Heinisch, *Theology of the Old Testament*, trans. William Heidt (Collegeville, Minnesota: Liturgical Press, 1950), p. 94.

mercy are more important, the notion of strength or steadfastness is in the word from the earliest times and is truly characteristic of it.

The Greek and the Latin translations of *hesed, eleos* and
misericordia, respectively, can be quite accurately translated by
the English word "mercy." But mercy, rather than being a part
of *hesed,* seems to spring from it. God will have mercy on man's
weakness, but the real source of the bond and the mercy that
results is *hesed.* Mercy is connected with fidelity in that both
are oriented toward the sinner. God, Who is faithful to His
promises, has assured the penitent of forgiveness. But the relationship of fidelity to mercy appears to be one of cause to effect.
Although mercy invariably follows after fidelity, it is not as
much a part of it as is love or faithfulness.

Although *hesed* means both love and faithfulness, and both
concepts are of equal importance, it is perhaps best to consider
the two notions separately. Scholars question our modern idea
of the character of the God of the Old Testament with regard
to His love for man. Too often, they feel, we tend to set up our
concept of God in the New Testament in opposition to that of
the old order. But this is an exaggeration of the division between the Old Law and the New Law, placing too much importance on the change of emphasis brought about through the
historical revelation of God's love. It is true that the emphasis
in the Gospels is more on the love of God the Father (and Son)
for mankind, but to fail to consider the love of Yahweh is an
injustice. Yahweh, the God of communion, was revealed as loving in His *hesed.* Furthermore, the *hesed* of the Old Testament
is more than merely love for those whom the law spoke of as
being justified—God's love includes both the just and the
wicked. God's love is a love for the whole nation of Israel, and
through the covenant this love is to be extended to the entire
human race.

In the Scriptures, especially in Hosea, Jeremiah, and Isaiah,
the *hesed* of God is often equivalent to His tender love for man.
We note this in the text of Jeremiah, which uses *hesed* and love

synonymously: "With an everlasting love have I loved you,
Therefore with [*hesed*] will I draw you to me" (31:3). Although
not as ready to connect *hesed* with justice, authors note that
hesed is *above* justice. Just as God's office involves judging man,
so His *hesed* is ever disposed to love man. But how can this be
the transcendent God of Israel, the Pillar of Fire, the In-
habitant of the Holy of Holies? On the natural level there can
be no equal intercourse between God and man, but communion
between God and man is possible by God's gracious initiation
of loving intercourse.[5] It was revealed to Israel that God de-
sired to have intercourse with man. For God is merciful and
gracious, long-suffering and abundant in love (*hesed*). This is
the God who first revealed Himself to Moses as being abundant
in *hesed,* indicating a love based on a firmly established relationship. It is precisely this fact of a relationship actually existing between God and Israel that brings out the love of God
so clearly. The writers of the historical narratives, the com-
posers of the Psalms, and the prophets all assume, again and
again, the reality and constancy of God's true and faithful love.
Isaiah was conscious of the faithful love of God, extolling it as
precious beyond anything else (Isa. 6:9). For Jeremiah, God's
faithful love became more meaningful in terms of his own love
for his wandering son. In the sense that *hesed* meant strength
or solidarity, it has been described as parallel to the knowledge
that comes from sexual intercourse. Both the analogies of love
for a straying loved one and the union of marriage are strik-
ingly combined in the prophet Hosea. Although he loved and
married a prostitute who was continually unfaithful to him,
his love for her never ceased. And so he could measure the love
of God for faithless Israel in terms of his own sad experience.

   But the *hesed* of God cannot be viewed as a mere fact, com-
forting as it may be. It has to be grasped in the context of a
history which sees the faithlessness of Israel repeated again and

---

[5] Theodorus C. Vriezen, *An Outline of Old Testament Theology* (London: Basil
Blackwell & Mott, 1958), p. 163.

again over against God's fidelity. For the *hesed* of God is not the *hesed* of men; it is eternal, always waiting for Israel. It is God's abiding faithfulness to Israel even when Israel ignored the covenant. Some consider *hesed* to have the primary meaning of determined faithfulness to a covenant. But before we speak of the covenant, it would be well to consider the faithfulness itself. As early as the accounts of Abraham do we find a firm, established union between God and man. This union or faithfulness is typified by the relationship of God to Abraham. In manifesting Himself to Moses, He is ". . . a God compassionate and gracious, slow to anger, abounding in kindness and fidelity, showing kindness to the thousandth generation . . ." (Exod. 34:6-7). The meanings of love and faithfulness are practically indistinguishable here because they are in fact complementary. Love would be meaningless without the quality of constancy that makes it never-failing. It is not that God must always be self-consistent, and thus faithful, in order to be God. Rather, He *is* God, unchanging in His love and, thus, faithful. This unchangeability of God's love is realized in both Deuteronomy (32:4) and Psalms (30:6). Hosea, who was so quick to recognize the agony of Yahweh's love for His faithless bride, Israel, also called Him the *faithful* Holy One (Hos. 11:12). Thus one must, above all, consider *hesed* in the historical context of God's dealing with Israel. In the history of Israel it was through a covenant that God showed His love and faithfulness. It may be helpful then to trace, in brief, the relation of *hesed* to the covenant.

There is another Hebrew word for the graciousness or favor that is shown through *hesed* in the covenant. That word is *hen,* and it stands for the favor shown by a superior to an inferior, a favor that is not given by right. Both qualities are part of the concept we have been studying; nevertheless, *hen* is quite different from the notion of *hesed*. *Hesed* is more closely connected with the idea of the covenant and, as we have shown, has a strong suggestion of fixedness, steadfastness, and determined loyalty. Essentially, *hesed* is a covenant word. We see here the primitive meanings of a relationship between two persons, such as that of mutual friendship within a nomadic society. It took Israel a long time to realize that her worship of Yahweh was not necessary for His existence. Yet even after this realization the idea of a reciprocal agreement or covenant remained. God's fidelity to Israel is conditioned upon the existence of a covenant, for God has bound His faithful love to Israel, and *hesed* is, at the same time, the means of the covenant's continuance. It does not follow, however, that the introduction of the idea of the covenant lessens to any extent the importance of the notion of love that is included in *hesed*. We remember the prophets who were consumed with the idea of the covenant with Israel as the token of God's love. If Israel shared in anything, it was a sense of community. The nation of Israel was bound to God not by some *impersonal* contract, but by the personal relationship of a covenant. For them, *hesed* had first meant the bond of man to man; after that it was the bond of God to man which made the community of Israel meaningful.

Within the community of the covenant, *hesed,* to the extent that men could share in it, imposed a double duty: that of giving to each man the share to which he had a right, and that of rendering to Yahweh the honor which was His due. Thus the distinction between the *hesed* that is essentially God's and the *hesed* in which man shares is blurred. *Hesed* becomes the means, through justice, of uniting man to man. It might seem natural to suppose that *hesed,* understood as the love of God, would have spread to all men, beginning from the basis of love's origin, or would have instituted justice to one's fellow man, which was required of the people of the covenant. But this never came about, for the covenant was continually transgressed by a faithless Israel. And so we are led to another aspect of the notion of *hesed,* that is, that it does not depend upon the good faith of the people.

We have already seen this aspect stressed from personal experience: what it meant to have a loved one stray and still be willing to forgive her. How much more loving, then, would God be, if a mortal can be so propitious? Scholars have pointed out, for instance, the conviction of Ezekiel that the faithlessness of the people does not cancel the faithfulness of God. Moreover, in Israel, belief in the love and faithfulness of Yahweh was so great that the possibility of forgiveness was never doubted. The basis of such belief was the fact that God had created His people and mantained a constant love for them, and, therefore, forgiveness was always waiting for them.

The quality of *hesed* that is the last to be considered is the natural result of Israel's experience of forgiveness, that is, the realization of the wonderfulness of God's fidelity. Some have seen an anticipation of Christian grace in a *hesed* that is the virtue of superiors and kings, and thus is purely gratuitous. Israel, especially when it had sinned, had no right to *hesed*. Since God is always righteous to the utmost, His fidelity surpasses wonder when He is merciful and loves, despite Israel's sinfulness. What is astonishing is not that He is loving and compassionate, but that His love is so unchanging, so firm, so utterly reliable. The gods of the pagans might love, but never with this constancy.

THE SAVING
GOD

✠ ✠ ✠ ✠

CHAPTER   NINE

The theme of salvation permeates the entire Old Testament. In order to understand its relation to the divine plan it will be well to trace its development through the various periods.

Salvation, when used in the Old Testament, is a word capable of many interpretations. Its significance ranges, on the national level, from spiritual progress to military victories. Yahweh saved Israel from slavery in Egypt, from famine and pestilence, and from the humiliating exile in Babylon. In the person of Moses He led the Hebrew people from the captivity of Egypt and prevented their perishing in the desert. Moses, too, is a savior in another way. He taught the people the will of Yahweh and brought them back from sin and idolatry when they had forsaken Yahweh.

Throughout Israel's history God raises up a host of "saviors" to educate and redeem His people from ignorance and folly. The great judges of Israel were leaders who saved the people of God from disastrous decisions. They mediated the covenant of Yahweh to Israel. The kings of Israel, too, acted the part that God has assigned them as His representatives and preserved justice and judgment in the land. And the prophets continued this process of education and salvation, precisely on the basis of their conviction that Yahweh would save His people.

When a modern reader studies the Old Testament, he discovers a concept which is totally strange to him. In pre-Exilic Israel, the unit for moral and religious purposes was not the individual but the group to which he belonged—family, community, or nation. Yahweh was considered primarily the God of Israel and only in a secondary sense the God of the individual Israelite. There was, of course, individual religion but it was "funneled" through the society to which the individual belonged. This funnel between God and the individual Jew was the corporate personality of the nation.[1]

We find a striking example of this phenomenon in the Book of Joshua:

> Then Joshua, accompanied by all Israel, took Achan,
> the descendent of Zerah, and the silver, the mantle,
> the bar of gold, his sons, his daughters, his oxen,
> his asses, his sheep, his household, and all that
> belonged to him, and they brought them to the valley
> of Achor.
>
> —JOSHUA 7:24

We see in this case how the whole family was punished for the sin of the father. This is no isolated instance in early Israel but an exemplification of a principle that was held generally and that had the full approval of Yahweh:

> . . . . For I, the LORD your God, am a jealous God,
> punishing children for the sins of their fathers, to the
> third or fourth generation of those who hate me. . . .
>
> —EXODUS 20:5

When we ask why God should save His people, we receive not one but several answers. The first answer is that whether Israel be morally good or morally bad, she is bound to Yahweh by the

---

[1] H. Wheeler Robinson, *The Religious Ideas of the Old Testament* (London: Gerald Duckworth & Co., Ltd., 1952), p. 87.

covenant. He loves Israel because He has bound Himself to the
fathers by an oath that He wishes to keep. The second answer
is that He chooses to save Israel for His name's sake, to punish
the wickedness of the nations, and to make clear His position
as Lord of history. Deuteronomy, it is true, presents Israel's
salvation as a consequence of her repentance. When Israel
sinned, she was punished, and when she repented, God inter-
vened to save her. But in the earlier narratives, God saves Israel
because she is *His*. The prophets underscored the close connection between Israel's sins and her suffering, and this idea gradually became dominant in later Old Testament thought. The
corporate personality that is Israel will be saved because God
will intervene to show her the error of her ways and, by not
sparing the rod, will educate the child to justice and so bring
about her salvation. He will achieve the final victory over sin
and initiate the kingdom of peace. The Old Testament's conviction that Yahweh is a saving God points hopefully to an ideal
that will be fulfilled in the New Testament, in the person of
One who completes Israel's destiny and realizes her hopes.

It is not, however, with the salvation of Israel as a whole but
rather with individual salvation and redemption that we are
presently concerned. Admittedly the idea of the individual's
salvation from sin and suffering occurred rather late in Old
Testament development. The idea of the group or corporate
nation was primary for many centuries. We do not find full
and explicit recognition of individuality in the Old Testament
until the publication of the Deuteronomic Law: "Fathers are
not to be put to death with their children, nor are children to
be put to death with their fathers. Everyone is to be put to
death for his own sin" (Deut. 24:16).

It is in Isaiah that we come upon the beginning of the stress
on individual salvation. In order to preserve and perpetuate his
teachings, Isaiah collected a group of disciples and gave them
written transcripts of certain of his oracles. In this way he not
only passed on his teaching but also separated from the corrupt
populace a small body of true believers, and thus anticipated in

a vague way individual salvation, substitution of a church for the nation, and separation of the redeemed from the worldly mass of apparent believers. As a result Isaiah has been said to have laid the foundation stone of both Judaism and Christianity.[2]

It is only toward the end of the seventh and the beginning of the sixth centuries, however, that we find a forceful stress being laid on the individual. The proponents of this emphasis are Ezekiel, Habakkuk, and Jeremiah. Thus, we find in Ezekiel a clear expression of the principle of individual responsibility:

> Why should not the son bear the consequences of his
> father's iniquity? If the son do what is lawful and
> right by being careful to observe all my statutes,
> he shall surely live.
>
> —EZEKIEL 18:19

Jeremiah made perhaps the most notable contribution to the principle, since he was himself intensely individualistic, a fact apparent in his relation with Yahweh. We also find in Jeremiah the prophecy of the "New Covenant" that Yahweh will make with the individual Israelite:

> But this is the covenant which I will make with the
> house of Israel after those days, is the oracle of the
> LORD: I will put my law within them, and will write it
> on their hearts; and I will be their God, and they shall
> be my people. And they shall teach no more every one
> his neighbor, and every one his brother, saying, know
> the LORD; for all of them shall know me, from the
> least of them to the greatest of them, is the oracle
> of the LORD: for I will pardon their guilt, and their
> sin will I remember no more.
>
> —JEREMIAH 31:33-34

This "New Covenant" is the antithesis of the Deuteronomic covenant with the nation as a whole that had failed of its purpose:

[2] Robert H. Pfeiffer, *Introduction to the Old Testament* (New York: Harper & Row, Publishers, 1948), p. 437.

Thus says the LORD: Stand by the ways, and look, and
ask for the ancient paths, where the good way is, and
walk in it; and find rest for yourselves. But they said:
We will not walk in it. So I set watchmen over them,
saying, Give heed to the sound of the trumpet. But
they said, We will not give heed. Therefore hear, O
heavens, and learn well what shall befall them! Hear,
O earth; for behold, I am bringing trouble upon this
people, the fruit of their own devices, because they
have not given heed to my words, and have spurned my
instruction. What care I for the frankincense that
comes from Sheba, or the sweet cane from a distant
land? Your burnt-offerings are not acceptable to me,
and your sacrifices bring me no pleasure. Therefore,
thus says the LORD: Behold, I am laying stumbling blocks
before this people, and they shall stumble against them,
fathers and sons together, and shall perish, both
neighbor and friend.

—JEREMIAH 6:16-21

Some biblical scholars feel that Jeremiah is not instituting a
personal religion to substitute for the national one but, in the
manner of the Deuteronomic Law, is directing his message to
the nation. According to this opinion, his oracles to individual
priests, prophets, kings, and friends are generally private in
character and personal in scope, without close connection with
his religious program as a whole.

With the growth of individualism the prophets no longer
serve as intermediaries between Yahweh and the nation but
between Yahweh and the individual.[3] God so loved the individual as to give him penitence and to save him through His
emissaries. While instructing the watchman in his duty, He
gave the following insight into the justice of His ways:

And if I say to the wicked man: You shall surely
die; and he turn from his sin, and do what is lawful
and right—if the wicked man restore the pledge,
repay what he has taken by robbery, follow the statutes

---

[3] Henry St. John Hart, *A Foreword to the Old Testament* (London: Adam &
Charles Black, 1951), p 80.

> that lead to life, and do no wrong, he shall surely
> live, and not die. None of the sins which he has
> committed shall be remembered against him; because he
> has done what is lawful and right, he shall surely live.
>   —EZEKIEL 33:14-16

According to Jeremiah, Yahweh will not consider the worshipping community as a whole, but will deal separately with each individual. The condition of His relation with these individuals will be the forgiveness of sin.

Ezekiel, on the other hand, a priest before he had been a prophet, included in his "New Covenant" a special class of priests necessary to ensure the sanctification of the people. In this way he combined the prophetic and priestly traditions in old Judah and transmitted them to the Second Temple.

Having seen how the notion of the individual developed in the Old Testament, we may now briefly consider the concurrent development of the idea of God's love and redeeming grace.

Because Israel's faith in God's mercy was so great, she did not doubt that He would find a means to forgive even the individual sinner, if he repented. God desires, not the death of His creatures, but their conversion. The *hesed* of God keeps Him bound to the Israelite, His kinsman, whom He is pledged to save. At times He may pour forth His anger and punish the wayward, but this is momentary. It almost seems to cost God something to punish the sinner.

The Psalms appeal to God to take the initiative in regenerating man spiritually. God is not aloof in the salvific process, for salvation is the evidence of the divine love in action upon the stage of history. As the Jews learned the true meaning of salvation, they spoke about it in terms of the love, the mercy, or the grace of God.[4]

God loved Israel, despite her unfaithfulness, and because of this love He forgave all transgressions. In the Hebrew Bible the

---

[4] Otto Baab, *The Theology of the Old Testament* (Nashville: Abingdon Press, 1949), p. 126.

word commonly used to denote this forgiving love for His people is *hesed,* the love of God, which reaches out in grace, mercy, and redemptive power. This love is extended to all who have sorrow for their sins and seek redemption: "Recall not the sins of my youth and my transgressions; according to thy mercy remember, me, on account of thy goodness, O Lord" (Psalms 25-7).

Yahweh is a strong and powerful God, but He is faithful to those that love Him:

> Who can stand before his wrath? Who can endure his
> fierce anger? His fury is poured out like fire, And
> the rocks are burst open by him. The LORD is good to
> those that wait for him. A stronghold on the day of
> trouble; He knows those that take refuge in him.
> —NAHUM 1:6-7

How exactly does redemption occur in the individual? The classical salvific pattern is as follows: First, there is the overpowering awareness of God coming to judge the individual:

> I saw the Lord, standing upon the altar, and he said:
> Smite the capitals, so that the thresholds may shake,
> and smash them on the heads of them all; and what may
> be left of them I will slay with the sword; not a single
> one of them shall get away, nor shall a single one
> escape. Though they dig into Sheol, Thence shall my
> hand take them; and though they mount up to the heavens,
> thence will I bring them down.
> —AMOS 9:1-2

Next there is the soul-searing realization of the degradation of human sin in the face of Almighty Majesty and Justice, followed by repentance and contrition. Repentance involves more than mere sorrow for sin. It also includes self-indictment and turning toward a new way of life in which sin will be absent. "Return, O rebellious Israel, saith the Lord, and I will not turn my face from you, for I am holy, saith the Lord, and I will not be angry forever."

Repentance is followed by dedication to a life of loyalty and

obedience to God. With renewed faith and will, the repentant
sinner sets out to do God's bidding:

> You have been told, O man, what is good, and what
> the LORD requires of you: only to do justice, and to
> love kindness, and to walk humbly with your God.
>   —MICAH 6:8

Walking solicitously "with your God" consisted of both private religious exercises and public ceremonies. Private religious
exercises were usually prayers, either formal or spontaneous. It
is interesting to note the sheer exultation which prayer brought,
the delight in the communion with the Lord:

> So have I beheld thee in the sanctuary, while
> seeing thy power and thy glory. Because thy kindness
> is better than life, My lips do praise thee.
>   —PSALM 63:3-4

These, in brief, are the stages of personal redemption in the
Old Testament; the human heart, previously callous to admoni-
tion, will henceforth belong to God.

The experience of salvation in the Old Testament is still a
relative thing, according to some scholars, and is quite different
from salvation in the New Testament.[5] According to the Old
Testament, peace of mind is provided with respect to individual
sins, but no permanent state of reconciliation is established.
The believer in the Old Testament was "pacified" concerning
the past, so as to begin anew in his attempt to be just through
the works of the law. Conversion, in the Old Testament, was
indeed received as a moral change, but not as a new creation.
There is also the further difference that in the Old Testament
the being of grace as an objective, transforming reality, which
is interior to the repentant sinner, was not clearly revealed.
Even the highest communion between God and man in the Old
Testament, that which was established with the prophets, does

---

[5] Gustav Oehler, *Theology of the Old Testament* (New York: Funk & Wagnalls
Co., 1888), p. 462.

not manifest that clear consciousness of sonship manifest in the New Testament: "Amen I say to you, among those born of women there has not risen a greater than John the Baptist; yet the least in the kingdom of heaven is greater than he" (Matt. 11:11).

But Israel never doubted that the time would come when God would establish His final kingdom of justice and peace. Even the psalms of the suffering poor presume that one day Yahweh will help, for He is righteous. However terrible the present situation, it will not last forever. Yahweh will one day be King of a perfect realm. Israel's hope is always turned to that future whose fulfillment will be in the person of the Savior, so long foreshadowed in word, whose work lies outside the scope of the Old Testament.

GOD
THE LORD
OF HISTORY

✠ ✠ ✠ ✠

CHAPTER TEN

In Israel's belief Yahweh was the Lord not only of Israel but of all the universe, its men and events: He was the Lord of history, which He guided toward its appointed end, the kingdom of the future, suavely but forcefully. It is this primordial conviction that aids Israel in giving to history a meaning and intelligibility unique among ancient peoples. The type of history preferred by the Hebrew historian might best be called "salvation-history." In this style of writing the past is not simply described for its own sake, but rather to point out the actions of God in history. That the personality of the author cannot be banished from his account of history has become a truism today. The concept of a totally "objective" history has been rejected as impossible. The past cannot be reconstructed exactly as it was, as Ranke and the great German objectivists would have liked. Granted this truth, we can accept more readily two cardinal features of Hebrew historiography: the selection of details according to a set criterion, and the primacy of interpretation over events.

The modern, scientific historian feels unhappy if he cannot

locate an event precisely as to when and where it happened. The Israelite historian felt less preoccupation with the past for its own sake. He was writing salvation-history and not simply a straightforward, factual account of what happened. The traditions of the past were recounted only to afford man the opportunity to see Yahweh at work modeling events to His purpose. The underlying meaning, the religious interpretation, of the event is what was stressed. Modern historians have learned, however, that the Hebrew storytellers' accounts are far more accurate than was once imagined. The Hebrew historian was neither indifferent to fact, nor desirous of distorting it. He weighed it for its theological significance.[1]

The fact that history was recorded at all in Israel is ample testimony to the existence of some unifying force and, consequently, some criterion for what is historical. History only develops for a reason, and it is obvious that by far the greater part of the Old Testament is a recording of history. In all the ancient Eastern world it is only in Israel that a true historical sense developed so early. This remarkable fact surely demands a background of a spiritual nature to explain Israel's concept of the unity of all human experience. That background can only be Yahwism—belief in the God Who has entered history and Who rules and decides the course of events. Because Israel felt the need to testify to the greatness of Yahweh, historiography arose to recount, demonstrate, and preserve the story of His will and activity.[2]

Because of the religious foundation of Israel's history, a selection of the events to be related was inevitable, as was a certain priority of interpretation over events themselves. Scholars have noted that as a general rule history is written under the guidance of unusual events that provide a turning point in the history of a people and force reflection about its past upon a na-

---

[1] Frederick L. Moriarty, *Introducing the Old Testament* (Milwaukee: Bruce Publishing Co., 1960), pp. 3-4.
[2] Theodorus C. Vriezen, *An Outline of Old Testament Theology* (London: Basil Blackwell & Mott, Ltd., 1958), pp. 227-88.

tion, and that can be grouped into two general categories: a peak of power and well-being, and great national calamities. That this is so in the Old Testament is obvious.

Yet these events alone do not constitute history. The reflection occasioned by the event is even more important than the facts, for it is the interpretation of an event that answers for its quality as an historical fact, that is, as a decisive fact in the course of history. Although the interpretation of an event will depend upon the interpreter, and the meaning given to it several centuries later may be a somewhat different one, this in no way lessens the value of history. For the interpretation is a reality equal to the event itself. The Israelite viewed God's action through faith and not through the methods of the archivist or the archaeologist.[3]

We turn now to the most dominant element in Hebrew theology—the conception of the revelation of God through history. While a general awareness of divine revelation in history may be present in many religions, it plays an unusually central role in Old Testament theology, not only because God intervenes frequently but also because of the directness of this intervention and His communion with man. Since Israel's belief in God seems to be wholly based on the experience of this divine activity, the background against which the image of God stands out in the Old Testament is history. There Yahweh is the God of history rather than the Creator or the God of Nature, although these elements are present also.

The most important note of God's self-revelation is its gradual character. God does not reveal Himself totally either at the beginning of history or at any single point. In many other ancient cultures God was believed to have revealed Himself in history; but the revelation actually took place in mythical time. At the beginning of the world, everything had taken place, all had been revealed, down to the least physiological, sociological,

---

[3] G. Ernest Wright, *The Challenge of Israel's Faith* (London: S.C.M. Press, Ltd., 1954), p. 42.

and cultural details: the creation of the world, and that of man, and his position in the cosmos. In the Old Testament, however, the revelation takes place in time. The Law is given to Moses, in a certain place, at a certain date. It is thus no longer reversible, and so it is more precious. In making use of the continuity of history God has made the time factor serve His purpose.[4]

In order to serve the purpose of Yahweh, time had to be conceived in a far different light among the Hebrews than among other ancient Eastern cultures. The traditional view of time was that of a cycle continually repeating itself. History was an infinite chain of cyclical periods, with very little change between the beginning and the end. The yearly cycle in nature was used as the prime model for all of history. The Hebrews, however, discovered a one-way view of time—a linear conception of history. This was a necessary result of their view of the continuing and purposeful revelation of God. Thus a goal was discerned in the history of the world, because history was enacted in a significant connection. The development of these ideas and their ultimate effect on the religious life of the Hebrews constituted a theocentric conception of history that completely dominated Israel's outlook upon life and fostered new theological insights. There is joy in faith and hope in the future, for the theocentric outlook upon life leads to the idea of theocracy in the life of the people and to teleology in the conception of history, which in turn leads to the belief in the restoration of Israel, the Messianic kingdom, the kingdom of salvation for the whole world, cosmic renewal, and finally to the ideal of the resurrection from the dead. Because God's work was brought into connection with this world and with the reality of everyday life, the religion of the Old Testament was saved from the dangers of exaggerated mysticism, other-worldliness, and con-

---

[4] Edmund Jacob, *Theology of the Old Testament,* trans. A. W. Heathcote and Philip J. Allcock (New York: Harper & Row, Publishers, 1958), p. 194. Cf. Mircea Eliade, *Cosmos and History* (New York: Harper & Row, Publishers, 1954), p. 105.

tempt for the values of this life, which elsewhere formed a
threat to man's spiritual life and kept his spiritual and his
natural life somehow opposed.[5]

This linear view of history also played an extremely important part in explaining to the Hebrew people the continual
catastrophes that befell them. History was advancing, but in an
undulating fashion—there were continually to be valleys of
tears. Suffering was borne because it was given by God, because
it was necessary for the final salvation of the people of Israel.
Calamities were not absurd or in vain, but were punishments
meted out by Yahweh because the chosen people had strayed
from the path of the righteous (which they seem to have done
with some regularity). The chosen people achieved almost no
material well-being and won almost no military victory that did
not eventually result in a sin that made punishment necessary.
All this punishment was foreseen and permitted by God to ensure that His people should not go against their true destiny
by alienating the religious heritage left to them by Moses. Suffering thus takes on a significance that is new in the ancient
world, because it is not the result of chance or fate but a necessary atonement for sin. And history itself becomes for the Jews
a series of deliverances, issuing from a series of judgments,
which anticipate the great final judgment.[6] So it was important
to the prophets to show that disasters, deserved or not, did not
invalidate the ancient covenant and that God's plan was simul-
taneously accomplished by destruction and construction. This
whole mystery was expressed by Isaiah in the following parable:

> Give ear, and hear my voice; attend, and hear my
> speech! Does the plowman keep plowing all the time,
> is he forever opening and harrowing his ground?
> Does he not, after leveling its surface, scatter dill,
> and sow cummin, and put in wheat and barley, with

[5] G. Ernest Wright, *The Old Testament Against Its Environment* (London: S.C.M.
Press, Ltd., 1957), p. 69.
[6] H. H. Rowley, *The Old Testament and Modern Study* (London: Oxford University Press, 1961), p. 292.

spelt as their border? For his God instructs and
teaches him aright. Dill is not threshed with a
threshing-sledge, nor is the wagon-wheel turned on
cummin; but dill is beaten with a staff, and cummin
with a flail. Is wheat crushed? No! one does not thresh
it forever, But when he has rolled his wagon-wheel over
it, he spreads it out, and does not crush it. This
also comes from the LORD of hosts, whose counsel is
wonderful, whose wisdom is great.
                                                    —ISAIAH 28:23-29

One could cite many examples of this sequence. But the
prophet's interpretation of the necessary character of these trib-
ulations for the reconciliation of Yahweh with the people of
Israel was far too difficult for the majority of the Israelites to
accept. It was easier to believe in accidents or negligence that
could be made up for with a ritual sacrifice. The alternation of
victory and defeat is one more confirmation of the importance
of history in the development of Hebrew religious experience
and its maintenance under high tensions. For the institutions
of prophecy and Messianism were, above all, validated by the
pressure of contemporary history.[7]

A further question raised by the Hebrew view of history is
the exact character of God's revelation in history. It is obvious
that the actions of God in history do not begin in the general
but in the particular. He chooses one small nation—a culturally
backward, nomadic tribe—which is eventually to influence all
nations and thus make the history universal. But for the present, history in general does not show the revelation of God in
direct acts. He does not step out of eternity for any other nation
or for all the nations as a whole. Yet we must be careful not to
limit the Hebraic conception of God to that of a tribal god. By
binding Himself to historic events, God shows His ultimate
concern with history and His direction of *all* history, for His
power does not end at the boundaries of a nation but directs

[7] George A. F. Knight, *A Christian Theology of the Old Testament* (London: S.C.M. Press, Ltd., 1959), p. 18.

universal history. Thus one may see in a declaration like that of Amos that Yahweh directs not only the destinies of Israel, but also that of the Philistines and the Ethiopians, a good illustration of the specific power of Israel's God. One can go further and say that God's presence was not always clearly revealed even with the history of Israel. He is present and thus her history is holy, but the events are not God's presence itself. The Hebrew's lively conception of God would not allow them to reduce it merely to events. Instead His presence in history is that of the hidden God Whose intentions always remain full of mystery in men's eyes. Yet He is also the one Who comes at certain moments in time to demonstrate through certain events the force of His being and action. The Hebrew would not allow God to be represented by a stone or wood image, nor even to be held static in thought or ideas, for his is a Living God Who acts.

A danger in this continual emphasis on the actual historical coming of God is the tendency to believe that man's actions are entirely predetermined. Yet this idea is not found in the Old Testament. Although history is seen as an unfolding of God's plan, man is left free to make decisions. This establishes a dialogue in which the two protagonists, God and man, call one another, flee from one another, and finally become reconciled. The problem of free will, however, did not have its full importance for the Hebrews at this time.

The relationship of history to faith in the Old Testament is fundamental. Some see positive and negative aspects to this demonstration of faith by history—the times of deliverance and the times of punishment, both being important for the development of faith. Others see the relationship more precisely as a double movement. On the one hand, history gives faith its object, an historical credo; on the other hand, faith gives to history its orientation through the prophets who bring, on Yahweh's behalf, the word that provokes or interprets events, and through the historians who envisage history in the light of God's plan of salvation taken as a whole and who consider only what was used in that plan's fulfillment as worth retaining for historical record.[8]

The revelation of God in history was primarily through the prophets. This is highly significant for the faith of Israel, for God often revealed to the prophets what He was about to do. When the events took place in time, they were simply a confirmation of what He had said. This gave the people a double motive of belief, each one set in history. And men believe because they see the events and also because they have heard the word of God through the prophets, and this word, they believe, has set the events in motion.

This continual intervention and revelation of God to the Hebrews makes it difficult to construct a systematic Old Testament theology. To seek for eternal, abiding truths in the Old Testament, which can then be arranged in categories and neatly strung together to form a system closed at both ends, is to ignore the way in which Hebrew theology developed. In the Old Testament there is little theorizing or purely abstract speculation. Rather there is observation of actual history in order that a warning and a lesson from God may be found for the guidance of the writer and His people. Hebrew theology is recitative; it is observable and discoverable in the historical unfolding of the purposes of God and becomes incarnate in, with, and through the working of God's Spirit upon the one nation, which in His wisdom Yahweh chose to use for His mighty purposes. Consequently, a theologian must try to follow in historical sequence the development of the relationship between the *living* God Who is spoken of so frequently in the Old Testament and the empirical people whom God has chosen to become His instrument for the attaining of His cosmic purpose.[9]

Israel created in her historical narratives a literary form unknown to the ancient near-East world. Her neighbors had no

---

[8] H. H. Rowley, *The Faith of Israel* (London: S.C.M. Press, 1956), p. 40.
[9] H. H. Rowley, *Rediscovery of the Old Testament* (Philadelphia: Westminster Press, 1946), pp. 128 ff.

concept of the historical process as a developing whole moving toward a definite term. The factor that lent intelligibility to the whole of history, in Israel's thought, was the action of God in human events and not the succession of brute events. Only the Hebrew evidenced this sense of history, and to him history was remarkable, not for its relation of the remembered past, but for the witness it bore to a theological truth: Yahweh is the supreme Lord of human events as He is of all other reality. Hebrew history is an interpretation of these events based upon the experience of Israel: God actively intervenes in the cause of history to lend it direction, and history, therefore, is the record of His salvific intentions. He is the Lord of history, the Savior, the Living and Present God.

APPENDIX: THE NAMES OF GOD

Note

Everything discussed in this appendix is problematic as it is difficult for Semiticists to reach agreement on the derivation of the names of God. We have included this appendix with some reservations; however, we feel it would be awkward to omit all mention of the names of God in the book, although we are sure that many scholars can be found to disagree with each of the statements made here.

THE NAMES OF GOD

The Israelites, as most primitive peoples, believed that the name of a person, in a certain sense, represented the essence of the person named. The name carried a *dunamis* or a force, acting upon the person and defining him. Hence, to know the name of a person was to know what, or, more properly, how he was, and, conversely, not to know his name was to know nothing of the person. In the case of God, to know His name is to know His nature as it was manifested to the Israelites. The name in its absolute significance is the divine Being as revealed, thereby making Himself intelligible to others.[1]

El

The generic name for God among all the Semitic peoples, with the exception of the Ethiopians, is formed on the root "el/ul" (cf. Allah). In Hebrew the root is represented by the form *El*. Various etymologies have been proposed for this root:[2]

---

[1] Edmund Jacob, *Theology of the Old Testament,* trans. A. W. Heathcote and Philip J. Allcock (New York: Harper and Row, Publishers, 1958), p. 43. Cf. Joseph Bonsirven, *Vocabulaire Biblique* (Paris: Lethielleux, 1958), p. 109.
[2] Paul van Imschoot, *Théologie de l'ancien testament* (Tournai: Desclée et Cie., 1954), I, 8-10.

1. It is derived from a root indicating the notion of "to be before," or "to be first."

2. It is related to the preposition "toward," in the sense of either "He toward whom one goes" or "He to whom one goes to render worship."

3. It is derived from a root indicating "strength" or "power." This root is also found in the word for "oak tree" and in the phrase "to be in the power of my hand" (Gen. 31:29).

4. It is related to a root indicating "to bind"; thus "He from whose power one cannot loose himself."

Of these etymologies, that which is derived from the root of "power" or "strength" is more generally accepted. From it, some derive the first notion, that of pre-eminence, as an ancillary notion to power, while others assimilate the notion of binding to that of power. The first interpretation of the second etymology, from the preposition "toward," is rejected by many on the grounds that it is too metaphysical for the primitive Israelites.

El may represent any god, or, more rarely, the one true God. In the latter case, it is almost always accompanied by the article or by a qualifying adjective.

Elohim

The most common generic name for God in the Old Testament is *Elohim*. This name, generally considered to be a plural form of El, gives the derivative of the poetic singular, *Eloah*. Some suggest that its root meaning is derived from "to be afraid," "to hide from"; thus Elohim is the object of terror and reverent fear, or at least should be. Some insist that this is the only meaning of Elohim, and, thus, by denying its relation with El, make it an exclusively Hebrew name for God. In agreement with most authorities we might assume that Elohim is simply the plural of El, though the notion of fear mentioned above may, through its parallel form, have played some part in the general conception of Elohim by the Hebrews.

Elohim, though plural in form, is always used with the singular article or adjective and a singular verb form when it is used in reference to the true God. As El, because of the broadness and uncertainty of its meaning, Elohim may also be used for specific gods of the Gentiles, and, as such, is often qualified by various compliments. The plural form should not be considered as referring to God and His angels, because of the singular verb which usually accompanies it and because the notion of angels is not prominent until the latter part of the Old Testament era. It has been suggested also that possibly the plural represents a pre-biblical polytheism, paralleled by other Semitic peoples, a plurality of forces which were later reunited into a superior, unique God. Thus Elohim would be considered as the sum of these previously disunited forces.

Against such a polytheistic interpretation, more conservative authors propose a plural of majesty, but such an idea is strictly a modern one, and kings in the Old Testament are always addressed in the singular. Others propose, on a parallel with Canaanite literature, that each shrine of God in a different locale may have had its own proper rites; the god thus worshipped would be considered as an originally different manifestation of God. Hence the plural would be indicative of an essential unity despite geographical diversity and would, thus, be on a grammatical parallel with such words as "water" and "sky" that are likewise in the plural, but indicate unity of nature despite diversity in their manifestations. However, it is quite possible that the plural is simply a plural of intensity, signifying the supreme transcendence of the God of Israel.

One should note also that Elohim is not specifically a proper name of God, but may also be applied to judges, kings, angels, the shades of the dead, and may even be used as a simple superlative.

El Elyon

El Elyon is not used exclusively as a term for the God of the Israelites, but is also found, for example, in the prayer of Melchisedech (Gen. 14:19), and was also known in Canaan and

Phoenicea. However, it occurs most frequently in Ecclesiastes.
The meaning of the adjective is traced to a root signifying "to
be lofty," whence is derived its commonly accepted meaning of
"the most high." This meaning is interpreted as applying to
the chief god, the *optimus maximus* of all Elohim. The title
expresses the transcendence of God, although the idea that He
dwells in Heaven is not entirely foreign to it either. Edmund
Jacob views El Elyon as an example of the general process of
unifying several gods under one chief god at Jerusalem, which
process would also be, he further explains, responsible for the
plural form of Elohim.[3] Whatever the origin of the term, its use
in the rest of the Bible indicates that the Israelites saw it as
another name for Yahweh.

El Shadday

Unlike El, Elohim, and El Elyon, *El Shadday* is used in the
Old Testament only in reference to the God of the Israelites. It
occurs primarily in the accounts of the Patriarchs and in Job
and has been variously interpreted:

1. It comes from the verb "to be powerful" or "to be vio-
lent." Thus, it would mean God in His might, as shown by
special deeds; or the absolute Mighty One Whom no one can
withstand and all can trust.

2. It is derived from a root meaning "the mountainous,"
hence, "sovereign," "lord," "highest," "assured refuge." [4]

3. It is related to the words "to water" and "breast," connot-
ing a notion of fertility, with the promise of the land of Canaan.

Yahweh

This name has been traced by some authorities to a cultic
exclamation "oh, He" by which God was hailed in religious
ceremonies. Even if this were so, it is certain that this simple
origin had been forgotten by biblical times.

---

[3] Jacob, *op. cit.*, p. 46.
[4] Theodorus C. Vriezen, *An Outline of Old Testament Theology* (London: Basil
Blackwell & Mott, Ltd., 1958), p. 197.

Yahweh is usually considered as the third person singular imperfect of "hawah," an archaic and more solemn form of "hayah," meaning "to be." The imperfect tense in Hebrew denotes a continuing action, whether past, present, or future. Hence, Yahweh would mean "He Who is, was, and shall be in the process of being." The problem lies in deciphering just what is implied in the meaning of "being."

The explanation of Exodus 3:14 as a refusal on the part of God to answer Moses, and thus to put Himself at the disposition of men, is doubtful. The revelation of God's name, and hence His nature, would not put God at the disposition of men, but would more likely increase their fear and awe in His presence. Moreover, nothing in the text suggests that Yahweh was avoiding the question. If He had chosen to refuse His name to Moses, He would have spoken more clearly. He has no fear that knowledge of His name would submit Him to magical constraint, for He is supremely transcendent.[5]

The Septuagint's rendering, *ho on*, "He who exists; He of whom the characteristic is existence," though upheld by some, has been rejected by most scholars on linguistic grounds. "Hayay" is much closer in meaning to the Greek *gignomai*, "become," than to *eimi*, "be." Moreover, such an explanation requires a turn of mind too metaphysical for the primitive Israelites.

Some authorities have also proposed a causative interpretation: "I will make what I will make." Thus, Yahweh would be announcing that He is above nature, being the Creator. This explanation is also probably too metaphysical, and, moreover, Yahweh was not primarily the Creator to the Israelites, but their King and Protector.

G. Oehler views "hayay" in the sense of becoming, as "God continually making Himself known in a process of historical revelation," as opposed to the concept held by pagan religions

---

[5] One of the best résumés of biblical scholarship concerning the name Yahweh may be found in the article by Myles M. Bourke, "Yahweh, The Divine Name," *The Bridge* (New York: Pantheon Books, Inc., 1958), III, 271-87. Cf. also Marvin H. Pope, *El in the Ugaritic Texts*, supplements to *Vetus Testamentum* (Leiden, The Netherlands: Brill, 1955), II.

that rely always upon past and completed revelation. Others suggest that the meaning of the word may be, "I am the God Who is ever present to you." But if God intended this to be the sole meaning of His name, He might well have chosen a name akin to Emmanuel, meaning "God is with us," which would have been much less cryptic. However, since existence is more a dynamic than a static concept to the Hebrew, when Yahweh asserts that He *is*, the notion of efficacious presence is also implied. Yahweh will be present as the ready helper of Israel. This is the traditional interpretation of the Talmud.

The name Yahweh must be understood as referring to Exodus 3:14, "I am Who am" or "I am what I am" or "I will be what I will be." Its true meaning must be sought in this phrase of self-identity, which suggests that God maintains Himself as what He is, thus indicating His sovereign freedom and independence in all domains. The identification, moreover, would suggest God's self-consistency, and, consequently, His immutability and eternity. From these attributes is derived the notion of Divine faithfulness: what God promises remains promised. This notion of fidelity appears to be latent in Exodus 3:15, which reads, "It is Yahweh, the God of your fathers, etc." God is the same to the Patriarchs and to Moses in that He is unchangeable, but in a moral and not a metaphysical sense. This notion of moral unchangeableness is of prime importance to Israel, forming the foundation of the covenant.

Was the name Yahweh a new name revealed to Moses? Or was it simply a name that had been in use before but was now adopted as the proper name of the natural God of Israel, the God of the covenant? Many deny the latter, citing the contrast between Yahweh and El Shadday in Exodus 6:2-3 as proof that Yahweh was a new name revealed to Moses by God. Nonetheless, the name Yahweh occurs often in the J tradition of Genesis and in the name of the mother of Moses in Exodus.

This apparent contradiction can be explained by the discovery of several distinct sources from which the writer of the Pentateuch had compiled his account. Thus, source E carefully avoids the use of Yahweh in favor of Elohim, until the revelation of this name to Moses, whereas source J uses the name throughout. Exodus 3:14 would be the account of God's revelation, according to source E, and source P would consider Exodus 6:2-3 as proof. R. Pfeiffer explains the presence of Yahweh in source J as resting upon the connection of the tribes of Judah with the Kenites and their familiarity with the Kenite god, which was related to Yahweh before the time of Moses and independent of him. Conversely, the tribes of Joseph became acquainted with Yahweh through Moses in Egypt, and source E thus preserves the northern tradition, according to which the name Yahweh was unknown to the Israelites before Moses. There are certain linguistic analogies that suggest some relation with non-Israelite gods, possibly through a general Semitic root for "god." Whereas we have no real evidence that a god of this name existed outside of Israel, we do know that it is very probable that the name Yahweh existed before Moses among the Patriarchs, but was slightly transformed by Moses to give it a new sense as the God of the Israelite nation. Hence, Exodus 6:2-3 could be explained as meaning that the Patriarchs did not have the full realization of the signification of this name as presented by Moses.

The absence of Yahweh from source E is probably attributable to stylistic considerations. The progressive revelation of God to the Israelites is paralleled by an evolution of His names in the epoch of the Patriarchs from Abraham to Moses: El, Elohim, El Elyon, El Shadday, and, in the final stage, Yahweh, where God reveals Himself as truly the God of His people. Elohim in source E is then the God of creation, transcendent, extending even to the heathen, and impossible to anthropomorphize. El Shadday is the God Who promises the land of Canaan, the God of the covenant, the ever-present God of the Hebrew theocracy.

This evolution in source E need not, however, correspond to the actual development of God's name. Indeed, some authorities conceive of a pantheon of household gods among the primitive Israelites dominated by Shadday, Who was eventually replaced by Yahweh; the cult of El, especially as El Elyon, emerged after being adopted from the Canaanites after the entrance of the Israelites into the Promised Land. But E, nonetheless, does present the evolution of God's relations with His people. It is the story of the universal God Who, in time, chooses the Israelites to be particularly His.

In any case, Yahweh is the personal name of God as revealed to the Israelites. As such, this name expresses in a certain manner the ineffable nature of God. In post-Exilic times, a sense of identity developed between this name and God Himself, leading to a fear of pronouncing the name. Thus, in the later books of the Old Testament, God is called almost exclusively *Adonay* or Elohim. Possibly the predominance of the name Elohim in the second book of the Psalms can be attributed to an editor who, possessed by this fear of the name of God, eliminated Yahweh from the text. For this reason, also, in sacred writings, the vowels of the word Yahweh were replaced by those of Adonay, "Lord," producing the familiar Jehovah.

Yahweh Sebaoth

Yahweh Sebaoth, the Lord of Hosts, does not appear as a title of God in the early books of the Old Testament. Also it had disappeared from usage by the time of the post-Exilic writings. This title of God seems to undergo a process of expansion as follows:

1. Yahweh Sebaoth is a war god and the leader of His people, Israel, in their fight against the Philistines. The hosts of Yahweh are the Hebrew people. However, the prophets, who use this expression most frequently, do not employ it in this primitive sense.

2. Yahweh has the host of heavenly bodies by which to aid His people. Thus, there is here added the notion of supremacy of Yahweh over the physical heavens. By some of the prophets, the expression, Lord of Hosts, was undoubtedly used to combat the idea that the stars were deities and to reaffirm Yahweh's position as Lord of all creation, including the stars.

3. The host of angels is likewise at the service of God. Hence,

there is here implied, in addition, the notion of Yahweh as the supreme spiritual entity.

This addition of meaning might parallel the development of Yahweh from a mere national god to the sole God of creation. Thus, in the final moment, Yahweh Sebaoth is conceived as Supreme God, the ruler Who controls the Israelites, the angelic hosts, and all earthly powers. He is, in short, master of heaven and of earth.

Adonay

Adonay, as we noted earlier, is used most frequently in the later books of the Old Testament as a substitute for the then feared name of God, Yahweh. It is formed from the word *adon,* "lord," as a plural of majesty, as a plural of abstraction, "my lordship," or as a frozen first person verbal form. Its earlier usage in Genesis is exclusively *adoni,* the vocative singular, showing that this name was originally conceived as a title of reverence and only later became an actual name of God. It is, in its general usage, a title indicating man's total belonging to God as his master: man is the slave of God, being dependent upon Him and under His absolute power and protection. In its original sense, however, it also recalls the fact that God, despite His transcendence, is in relation with His faithful people, ruling them absolutely, but heeding their prayers and deserving their gratitude.

Baal

Baal, the general word for "master," "lord," "possessor" in all the Semitic languages, is used in the Old Testament both as a common and a proper noun. As a common noun, it is used for an owner, for a husband, and in usage parallels the Roman *paterfamilias.* God is occasionally referred to both as the *paterfamilias* and, in Hosea, as the husband of the Israelite people. As a proper noun, Baal is the name of the male fertility god associated with the various local shrines of Canaan. These Baals, originally simply a plurality of manifestations of a single god associated with the goddess Astarte, had, before the arrival of the Israelites in Canaan, come to be considered as specific minor gods, each with his own cult, often orgiastic, and his own specialization.

Upon their entrance into the Promised Land, the Israelites in some way adopted these Baals, probably by assimilating their nature functions and their geographical diversity and multiplicity to Yahweh. The reason for this adoption can probably be traced to the new agricultural way of life that the Israelites had taken up. They learned agriculture from the Canaanites and, consequently, the nature attributes of their gods, the Baals. Another explanation of the acceptance of Baalism is that the Israelites considered their Yahweh more a war god, associated with past history, whereas the Baals were the fertility gods of their new way of life. Or perhaps the orgiastic rites of the Baals attracted the Israelites. This "Baalization" was fought by the prophets, notably Hosea, and its effects gradually diminished in the kingdom.

After the division of the tribes of Israel and of Judah, Jezebel, the Phoenician wife of Ahab, introduced her cult of Baalism to the ten tribes, in association with Yahwism. Even at this time, among the tribes of Judah, there were still traces of the ancient Canaanite Baal worship.

Thus, there are three distinct uses of the word Baal. The first is in reference to the orthodox Yahweh, paralleling the use of Adonay, which generally replaced Yahweh. The second use is in reference to the Canaanite Baals with which the Israelites, upon their entrance into the Promised Land, diluted their worship of Yahweh. The third reference is to the Phoenician Baal, imported into Israel by Jezebel.

Other Names of God

Melek is the word for "king" common to all Semitic languages. The adoption of the title is prior to the earthly kingdom of Israel, and its usage is most strong in the Exilic period.

It solidifies the notions of rule and presence to Israel implied in the title Yahweh. Particularly in the Exilic and post-Exilic periods, it insists upon the eschatological notion of God's kingdom and covenant.

The Holy One of Israel is a term devised and used by Isaiah, equating divinity with holiness, with the implication that God hates sin and demands a holy life.

Ab, signifying Father, is used to denote one who demands the respect of his children. Yahweh is called *Ab* because He is the Creator of His people. The Israelites rarely called Yahweh their father. Rather it was used by Yahweh Himself announcing His Creatorship and calling the Israelites His sons.

SUGGESTED READINGS

* Albright, William F. *From the Stone Age to Christianity.* New York: Doubleday & Company, Inc., 1957.
* ———. *Archeology and the Religion of Israel.* Baltimore: John Hopkins University Press, 1942.
* Anderson, Bernhard W. *Understanding the Old Testament.* Englewood Cliffs, N. J.: Prentice-Hall, Inc., 1957.
* Baab, Otto. *The Theology of the Old Testament.* Nashville: Abingdon Press, 1949.
Bonsirven, Joseph. *Vocabulaire biblique.* Paris: Lethielleux, 1958.
Charlier, Célestin. *The Christian Approach to the Bible.* Translated by Hubert J. Richards and Brendan Peters. Westminster, Md.: The Newman Press, 1958.
Dougherty, John J. *Searching the Scriptures.* New York: Doubleday & Company, Inc., 1959.
* Eichrodt, Walther. *Theology of the Old Testament.* Translated by J. A. Baker. Vol. I. Philadelphia: Westminster Press, 1961.
Gelin, Albert. *The Key Concepts of the Old Testament.* Translated by George Lamb. New York: Sheed & Ward, Inc., 1955.
Giblet, Jean, *et al. The God of Israel, The God of Christians.* Paris: Desclée et Cie., 1961.

Guillet, Jacques. *Themes of the Bible*. South Bend: Fides Publishers, 1960.

Heinisch, Paul. *Theology of the Old Testament*. Translated by William Heidt. Collegeville, Minnesota: Liturgical Press, 1950.

* Jacob, Edmund. *Theology of the Old Testament*. Translated by A. W. Heathcote and Philip J. Allcock. New York: Harper & Row, Publishers, 1958.

Jones, Alexander. *Unless Some Man Show Me*. New York: Sheed & Ward, Inc., 1960.

* Knight, George A. F. *A Christian Theology of the Old Testament*. London: S.C.M. Press, Ltd., 1959.

* Koehler, Ludwig. *Old Testament Theology*. Translated by A. S. Todd. Philadelphia: Westminster Press, 1957.

McKenzie, John L. *The Two-Edged Sword, An Interpretation of the Old Testament*. Milwaukee: Bruce Publishing Co., 1956.

Moriarty, Frederick L. *Introducing the Old Testament*. Milwaukee: Bruce Publishing Co., 1960.

————. *Foreword to the Old Testament*. Weston, Mass.: Weston College Press, 1954.

* Robinson, H. Wheeler. *The Religious Ideas of the Old Testament*. London: Gerald Duckworth & Co., Ltd., 1952.

* Rowley, H. H. *Rediscovery of the Old Testament*. Philadelphia: Westminster Press, 1946.

* ————. *The Faith of Israel*. Philadelphia: Westminster Press, 1955.

* ————. *The Old Testament and Modern Study*. London: Oxford University Press, 1961.

* Snaith, Norman H. *The Distinctive Ideas of the Old Testament*. London: The Epworth Press, 1957.

Sorg, Remberg. *Hesed and Hasid in the Psalms*. St. Louis: Pio Decimo Press, 1953.

Vawter, Bruce. *A Path Through Genesis*. New York: Sheed & Ward, Inc., 1956.

————. *The Conscience of Israel*. New York: Sheed & Ward, Inc., 1961.

————. *The Bible in the Church*. New York: Sheed & Ward, Inc., 1959.

* Vriezen, Theodorus C. *An Outline of Old Testament Theology*. London: Basil Blackwell & Mott, Ltd., 1958.

* Wright, G. Ernest. *The Old Testament Against Its Environment*. London: S.C.M. Press, Ltd., 1957.

* ————. *God Who Acts*. London: S.C.M. Press, Ltd., 1958.

* ————. *The Challenge of Israel's Faith*. London: S.C.M. Press, Ltd., 1954.

* Non-Catholic.